blue ginger

For mum and dad.

This book would not have been possible without the help of the following people: most importantly, my mum and dad for steadfastly supporting me over the years; Michael, a very supportive business partner who has allowed me the chance to do what I love; my loyal patrons—without them neither the restaurant nor the book would exist; and my staff for allowing me to take time off to do the book while they ran the restaurant.

Thanks also to the team at Murdoch Books for making my first book go so smoothly: Amanda for her dogged persistence in persuading me to write the book; Juliet for believing in me enough to allow me the chance to write this book; Kay, for her gracious support and patience; Marylouise for her beautiful design and creative vision; Zoë for being so easy to work with and her continual encouragement; Diana for editorial support; Katy for ensuring all the recipes work in the domestic kitchen; Ross for vigorous testing and preparing the food so well; and Christine and Mikkel, a fantastic team, who brought the food to life with their beautiful photography. Also, thanks to all those people behind the scenes who have helped make this book a reality.

Last but not least, to Amy who inspired me to become a better man and who provides the spark in my life.

Published by Murdoch Books® a division of Murdoch Magazines Pty Ltd.

Murdoch Books® Australia
Pier 8/9, 23 Hickson Road, Millers Point NSW 2000
Phone: +61 (0)2 4352 7000 Fax: +61 (0)2 4352 7026

Murdoch Books Ltd UK
Erico House, 6th Floor North, 93–99 Upper Richmond Road
Putney, London SW15 2TG
Phone: + 44 (0) 20 8785 5995 Fax: + 44 (0) 20 8785 5985

Chief Executive: Juliet Rogers
Publisher: Kay Scarlett

Photographer: Mikkel Vang Stylist: Christine Rudolph
Art direction and design: Marylouise Brammer
Editor: Zoë Harpham
Food editor: Katy Holder
Food preparation and testing: Ross Dobson
Editorial Director: Diana Hill
Production: Megan Alsop
Photographer's assistant: Matt Burke Stylist's assistant: Nina Ross

National Library of Australia Cataloguing-in-Publication Data
Huynh, Leslie, 1968- . Blue Ginger. Includes index. ISBN 1 74045 374 3
1. Blue Ginger (Restaurant: Sydney, N.S.W.). 2. Cookery, Asian.
3. Restaurants – New South Wales – Sydney. I. Title.
641.595

IMPORTANT: Those who might be at risk from the effects of salmonella poisoning (the elderly, pregnant women, young children and those suffering from immune deficiency diseases) should consult their doctor with any concerns about eating raw eggs.

The Publisher thanks Archaeos, Bison Homewares, Moss Melbourne, Mud Australia, Roost, Safari, Step Back and The Essential Ingredient for their assistance with the photography for this book.

blue ginger

les huynh

photography by Mikkel Vang
styling by Christine Rudolph

MURDOCH
B O O K S

contents

blue ginger

Like the striking blooms of the blue ginger flower, my food is colourful and fragrant. I've long believed that food that looks attractive and smells delicious stimulates the senses and the appetite. That's why I love Asian food—there are so many fresh herbs, intoxicating spices and vibrant colours that each meal is an explosion of sensation.

I am a largely self-taught chef with a varied background, so my recipes are an eclectic mixture. Some I learned during my childhood in Vietnam, some come from my Chinese parents and others from living and travelling in South-East Asia. Because I love to experiment when cooking, I've taken many of these traditional Asian recipes and adapted them to my new home by using local flavours and produce and relaxing the rules a little. Take the same approach yourself. If you can't get hold of one of the ingredients, replace it with something similar and then have fun with the cooking process. I hope you'll be blown away by the experience of cooking *Blue Ginger* style.

first

first

I've always loved snacks and starters in preference to main meals. This is partly because I find them more interesting to cook and partly because they are what I prefer to eat. Smaller portions of food not only allow for greater inventiveness but also provide more varied flavours. My ideal is to be presented with a colourful array of small dishes to nibble through gradually.

Traditionally, most Asian cultures don't serve starters in the formal European way. Food is brought to the table as soon as it's ready, which may mean that a plate of spring rolls sits adjacent to a steamed fish. But I know from my experience in the restaurant industry that many people prefer to be served a small meal before their main. The recipes in this chapter are designed so they can work either way—as part of a banquet or as an entrée. If you're serving these as part of a larger feast, choose two or more of the recipes from this chapter alongside a selection of mains. Consider adjusting the presentation so that rather than dividing the food among small plates, you serve it on a platter.

*   I like to make most of my own sauces, stocks and condiments, but many of these are also commercially available, so I've marked these ingredients with a star*. When you're starting out, you may prefer to use the ready-made variety. When you want to become fully involved in the process, you can go to the Basics section for recipes for making your own.

You can serve these as fingerfood by trimming the won ton skins to 5 cm (2 inch) squares before you fry them.

Crispy won ton skins topped with crab and lychee salad

vegetable oil, for deep-frying
1 packet won ton skins (you'll need about 12)

Dressing
1 garlic clove, peeled
3 red Asian shallots, peeled
3 tablespoons lime juice
2 tablespoons fish sauce
2 tablespoons caster (superfine) sugar

Salad
200 g (1 cup) cooked blue swimmer crabmeat
95 g (1/2 cup) finely diced tinned lychees
135 g (1 1/2 cups) bean sprouts, trimmed
4–5 spring onions (scallions), julienned on the diagonal
3 tablespoons finely sliced Thai basil leaves
1 long red chilli, deseeded and julienned
30 g (1 cup) coriander (cilantro) leaves

To serve
3 tablespoons salmon roe
3 tablespoons fried shallots* (optional)

Makes about 12

Fill a wok or deep-fat fryer one-third full of oil and heat to 180°C (350°F), or until a cube of bread dropped into the oil browns in 15 seconds. Gently lower two won ton skins at a time into the wok and cook until crisp on both sides. Drain thoroughly on paper towels.

To make the dressing, use a mortar and pestle to pound the garlic and shallots together. Work in the lime juice, fish sauce and sugar, pounding until the sugar dissolves. Alternatively, chop the ingredients into a paste using a small food processor.

To make the salad, combine all the ingredients and gently mix in a large bowl, then moisten with the dressing.

To serve, put a little of the crabmeat salad on top of each won ton skin, then add a little salmon roe on top. Sprinkle with fried shallots, if you wish.

Don't judge fresh water chestnuts by their dark, misshapen appearance—once they are peeled, the crunch of the sweetly flavoured flesh is sublime.

Chicken san choy bau

4 small iceberg lettuce leaves
50 g (1³/4 oz) bean thread vermicelli
vegetable oil, for deep-frying
2 tablespoons Shaoxing rice wine
1 tablespoon oyster sauce
2 garlic cloves, crushed
2 lap cheong (Chinese sausages), finely sliced
2 teaspoons finely grated fresh ginger
200 g (7 oz) minced (ground) chicken
5–6 baby corn, roughly diced
225 g (8 oz) peeled fresh or tinned water chestnuts, chopped
2 large oyster mushrooms, roughly sliced
5 spring onions (scallions), roughly sliced

Makes 4

Refrigerate the lettuce leaves until you're ready to use them.

Break up the vermicelli nest with your hands. Fill a wok one-third full of oil and heat to 180°C (350°F), or until a cube of bread dropped into the oil browns in 15 seconds. Deep-fry the vermicelli in small batches for 20–30 seconds, or until puffed and crisp. Drain on crumpled paper towels, then break into 6 cm (2¹/2 inch) lengths. Clean out the wok, reserving 2 tablespoons of the oil.

Mix the rice wine and oyster sauce together. Heat the reserved oil in a clean, hot wok, then stir in the garlic, lap cheong and ginger and stir-fry for 30 seconds. Add the chicken and stir-fry for 1 minute. Add the corn, water chestnuts and oyster mushrooms and stir-fry for 2 minutes. Next add the rice wine mixture, spring onions and a pinch of white pepper and stir-fry for a further 1 minute.

To serve, divide the chicken mixture among the lettuce cups and top with the fried vermicelli.

For a casual gathering, do as the Vietnamese do and put all the food on the table and have each person assemble their own meal. Put the salad ingredients on one plate, the sugar cane prawns on another and the lettuce leaves on a third.

Vietnamese sugar cane prawns on vermicelli salad

2 garlic cloves, roughly chopped
100 g (3¹/2 oz) minced (ground) fatty pork
400 g (14 oz) raw small prawns (shrimp), peeled and deveined
1 teaspoon sugar
1 teaspoon fish sauce
1 tablespoon ground roasted rice*
2 x 10 cm (4 inch) lengths of tinned sugar cane, each quartered lengthways
vegetable oil

Salad
100 g (3¹/2 oz) dried rice vermicelli
1 handful mint leaves
1 handful coriander (cilantro) leaves
1 carrot, finely julienned

To serve
4 or 8 small whole iceberg lettuce leaves
1 quantity nuoc cham (Vietnamese dipping sauce)*

Serves 4 or 8

Put the garlic and pork in a food processor. Process to a smooth paste. Add the prawns, sugar, fish sauce, rice powder and a pinch of salt and white pepper. Process until the mixture is smooth.

Wet your hands with a little oil, gather up some prawn mixture and mould it into a ball, approximately the size of a golf ball. Press the ball into the cup of your hand to create a small disc and wrap it around a piece of sugar cane so that it covers about 6 cm (2¹/2 inches) of the cane. Repeat with the remaining prawn mixture and sugar canes. Refrigerate for 5–10 minutes, or until firm. Lightly oil your fingers, then use them to smooth the prawn mixture.

Put the vermicelli in a bowl and cover with boiling water. Leave to soften for 5–7 minutes. Drain, refresh under cold water, then drain again. Combine the vermicelli with the rest of the salad in a bowl.

Preheat a chargrill pan or barbecue hotplate over medium heat. Cook the sugar cane prawns for 3–5 minutes, or until cooked, turning them regularly so they brown evenly.

To serve, divide the salad among the lettuce cups. Add one or two sugar cane prawns and accompany with some nuoc cham.

This is a surprisingly easy meal and it's great for a party because you can prepare most of it well in advance. In fact, the longer you leave the spatchcock in the fridge, the crispier the skin will become. When your guests arrive all you have to do is cook the spatchcock for a few minutes.

Twice-cooked spatchcock with herb salt

2 x 600 g (1 lb 5 oz) spatchcocks (poussins)
vegetable oil, for deep-frying

Stock
500 ml (2 cups) Shaoxing rice wine
10 garlic cloves, crushed
2 knobs of fresh ginger, bruised
1 onion, peeled
4 tablespoons salt
12 white peppercorns
2 tablespoons honey

To serve
2 tablespoons herb salt*
4 lime wedges

Serves 4

Put all the stock ingredients into a stockpot or very large saucepan with 6 litres (24 cups) water and bring to the boil. Rinse the spatchcocks under cold water, then pat dry. Lower the spatchcocks, breast-side down, into the simmering stock, making sure they are fully submerged. Poach for 5–6 minutes, then remove the pot from the heat. Cover with a tight lid and allow the spatchcocks to cool in the stock for 1 hour—they will continue to cook during this time. Carefully remove the spatchcocks from the pot. Put on a tray and refrigerate overnight—this dries out the skin.

Fill a wok or deep-fat fryer one-half full of oil and heat to 170–180°C (325–350°F), or until a cube of bread dropped into the oil browns in 15–20 seconds. Cut the spatchcocks in half through the breastbone and backbone. Deep-fry them, a few pieces at a time, for 2–3 minutes, or until golden brown. Drain on paper towels, then cut each piece into three smaller pieces. Serve with the herb salt and lime wedges on the side.

Cabbage adds a raw crunch to the salad, which complements the smokiness of the cashew nuts and ground roasted rice.

Thai minced chicken salad with cashew nuts

250 ml (1 cup) chicken stock* or water
500 g (1 lb 2 oz) minced (ground) chicken

Dressing
4 tablespoons lime juice
3 tablespoons fish sauce
1 tablespoon shaved palm sugar
1/2 teaspoon roasted chilli powder

Herb and nut mixture
1 handful mint leaves
1 handful coriander (cilantro) leaves
2 spring onions (scallions), sliced
4 red Asian shallots, sliced
1 lemon grass stem (white part only), very finely sliced
8 cherry tomatoes, halved
1 handful roasted cashew nuts*

To serve
2 tablespoons ground roasted rice*
4 large wedges of white cabbage

Serves 4

To make the dressing, combine the lime juice, fish sauce, palm sugar, chilli powder and a pinch of salt in a small bowl and stir until the sugar has dissolved.

To make the herb and nut mixture, combine all the ingredients in a bowl and gently toss them together.

Pour the chicken stock into a saucepan and bring to the boil. Add the chicken and a pinch of salt. Cook, stirring frequently, for 3–4 minutes, or until the chicken is just cooked, then drain and put in a large bowl. Add the dressing and all the herb and nut mixture to the chicken, then toss together thoroughly.

To serve, divide the chicken salad among four plates and sprinkle with ground roasted rice. Serve a wedge of cabbage alongside each plate.

When green mangoes aren't in season, you can use a small green papaya, though you may need to add a little more lime juice to the dressing.

Fried smoked salmon with green mango salad

vegetable oil, for deep-frying
300 g (10½ oz) hot-smoked salmon,
cut into 3 cm (1¼ inch) squares

Dressing
1 garlic clove, peeled
1 long red chilli, deseeded and chopped
2 tablespoons shaved palm sugar
2 tablespoons fish sauce
2 tablespoons lime juice

Salad
2 small green mangoes, peeled and julienned
3 red Asian shallots, sliced
1 long red chilli, deseeded and julienned
1 handful mint leaves
1 handful coriander (cilantro) leaves
2 tablespoons roughly chopped roasted peanuts*

To serve
4 x 12 cm (5 inch) square pieces of banana leaf

Serves 4

To make the dressing, use a mortar and pestle to pound the garlic, chilli and a pinch of salt together. Work in the sugar, fish sauce and lime juice, pounding until the sugar dissolves. Alternatively, chop the ingredients into a paste using a small food processor.

Fill a wok or deep-fat fryer one-third full of oil and heat to 170–180°C (325–350°F), or until a cube of bread dropped into the oil browns in 15–20 seconds. Deep-fry the salmon in small batches for 2–3 minutes each batch, or until golden and crisp. Drain on crumpled paper towels.

To make the salad, combine all the ingredients in a large bowl and mix together gently. Pour on the dressing. Use your hands to break up the salmon slightly and toss into the salad.

To serve, place a square of banana leaf onto each plate, then top with the salmon salad.

For a summer barbecue you can't go past this fresh Vietnamese salad with sizzling lemon grass prawns off the hotplate.

Chargrilled lemon grass prawns with Vietnamese salad

12 large raw prawns (shrimp), peeled and deveined, tails and heads left on

Marinade
2 garlic cloves, peeled
3 lemon grass stems (white part only), finely chopped
4 tablespoons peanut oil
1 tablespoon oyster sauce
1 teaspoon fish sauce

Dressing
2 garlic cloves, peeled
1 long red chilli, deseeded and chopped
2 tablespoons caster (superfine) sugar
3 tablespoons fish sauce
2 tablespoons lime juice
2 tablespoons rice vinegar

Salad
225 g (3 cups) shredded white cabbage
90 g (1 cup) finely julienned carrots
1 Lebanese (short) cucumber, thinly sliced into long ribbons
2 large handfuls Vietnamese mint leaves
2 large handfuls coriander (cilantro) leaves
80 g (1/2 cup) finely sliced onions
4 tablespoons roughly chopped roasted peanuts*
2 tablespoons fried shallots*

To serve
4 lime halves

Serves 4

To make the marinade, use a mortar and pestle to pound the garlic, lemon grass and a pinch of salt into a paste. Work in the rest of the ingredients and a pinch of white pepper, pounding until the sugar dissolves. Alternatively, chop the ingredients into a paste using a small food processor. Scoop the dressing into a non-metallic bowl with the prawns. Coat the prawns well, then marinate in the refrigerator for at least 1 hour.

Remove the prawns from the marinade. Heat a chargrill pan or barbecue hotplate over medium–high heat, then cook the prawns for 3–4 minutes on each side, or until cooked.

To make the dressing, use a mortar and pestle to pound the garlic and chilli together. Work in the sugar, then stir in the fish sauce, lime juice, rice vinegar and 2 tablespoons water, pounding until the sugar dissolves. Alternatively, chop the ingredients into a paste using a small food processor.

To make the salad, gently toss all ingredients together in a large bowl. Toss with enough of the dressing to moisten the salad.

To serve, divide the salad among four plates, then sit three prawns on top. Drizzle a little more of the dressing over the prawns. Add a lime half on the side.

This is an interesting take on the traditional frittata. By steaming rather than frying it, the consistency of the egg becomes soft and delicate, enhancing the subtle flavour of the crab.

Vietnamese steamed crabmeat frittata with watercress salad

Crabmeat frittata
3 large fresh or dried cloud ear fungus
5 g (1/8 oz) bean thread vermicelli
3 spring onions (scallions), sliced
8 eggs, lightly beaten
250 g (9 oz) cooked crabmeat

Salad
25 g (2 handfuls) watercress sprigs
1 quantity black vinegar dressing*

Serves 4–6

If you are using fresh cloud ear fungus, finely chop them. If using dried, first soak them in hot water for 20 minutes, then drain and finely slice. Soak the bean thread vermicelli in cold water for 10 minutes, or until softened, then drain and cut into 5 cm (2 inch) lengths.

Combine all the ingredients for the frittata in a bowl with 1/2 teaspoon salt and a pinch of white pepper. Gently stir until well combined. Pour the mixture into a 1.5 litre (6 cup) rectangular baking dish.

Bring a wok or large saucepan of water to the boil. Put the baking dish into a large steamer. Sit the steamer over the wok of boiling water, making sure the base of the steamer does not touch the water. Put the lid on the steamer and steam the frittata for 15–20 minutes, or until cooked through.

Remove the stems from the watercress and lightly dress the leaves in the black vinegar dressing—you may not need it all.

To serve, slice the frittata and serve each slice on a plate with some watercress salad and a pinch of white pepper. Serve warm or at room temperature. Best eaten on the day it is cooked.

I'm lucky to live near a fish market, so I buy locally sourced Balmain bugs off the trawler. The sweetness of the meat and delicate texture of live slipper lobsters make them well worth paying more for. But if you don't live near a fish market, most fishmongers sell frozen lobster meat.

Slipper lobsters with banana blossom salad

8 slipper lobsters (e.g. Moreton Bay or Balmain bugs) or scampi, thawed if frozen

Dressing
2 garlic cloves, peeled
1 long red chilli, deseeded and chopped
2 teaspoons grated fresh ginger
1 tablespoon sugar
2–3 tablespoons fish sauce
2 tablespoons lime juice

Salad
1 banana blossom
1 teaspoon white vinegar or lime juice
1 long red chilli, julienned
1 large handful Vietnamese mint leaves
1 handful coriander (cilantro) leaves
3 red Asian shallots, sliced

To serve
4 x 12 cm (5 inch) square pieces of banana leaf (optional)
3 tablespoons roasted peanuts*
2 tablespoons fried shallots*
4 lime wedges

Serves 4

Put the lobsters in a large saucepan and cover with water. Bring to the boil, then reduce the heat and simmer for 6–7 minutes, or until cooked. Drain and allow to cool. Cut into the membrane where the head and body join, to loosen, then twist or cut off the tail. Discard the head. Cut down on both sides of the underside shell, then peel back the soft shell to reveal the flesh. Gently pull the flesh out in one piece. Discard the shell. Chop the meat very roughly, then set aside.

To make the dressing, use a mortar and pestle to pound the garlic, chilli and ginger together. Work in the sugar, fish sauce and lime juice, pounding until the sugar dissolves. Alternatively, chop the ingredients into a paste using a small food processor.

To make the salad, start by preparing the banana blossom. Wearing gloves, remove and discard the outer coarse leaves from the banana blossom. Finely slice the remaining blossom on the diagonal. Put in a bowl of water with the vinegar or lime juice for 15 minutes. Drain and pat dry with paper towel, then put in a large bowl. Add the rest of the salad ingredients and the cooked slipper lobster meat. Toss well. Pour over the dressing and toss gently until well combined.

To serve, lay a piece of banana leaf on each plate (if using) and top with a mound of the salad. Sprinkle with the peanuts and fried shallots and serve the lime wedges on the side.

Beautiful, speckled quail eggs have a lusciously rich yolk, which contrasts with the subtle flavour of the chicken.

Coconut chicken salad with quail eggs

8 quail eggs
750 ml (3 cups) coconut milk
400 g (14 oz) chicken breast fillet

Dressing
1 garlic clove, peeled
1 tablespoon shaved palm sugar
2–3 tablespoons fish sauce
2 tablespoons lime juice
pinch of chilli flakes

Salad
1 handful bean sprouts, trimmed
1 handful Thai basil leaves
1 handful coriander (cilantro) leaves
4 makrut (kaffir) lime leaves, very finely shredded

To serve
2 tablespoons ground roasted peanuts*
2 tablespoons fried shallots*

Serves 4

Put the quail eggs in a small saucepan of water. Bring to the boil, then cook for 2 minutes. Drain and run under cold water. Peel and cut in half.

Heat the coconut milk and 1 teaspoon salt in a saucepan until simmering. Add the chicken and simmer gently for 6–7 minutes. Allow the chicken to cool in the coconut milk—it will continue to cook during this time. Remove the chicken from the liquid, reserving 1 tablespoon of the poaching liquid. Slice the chicken.

To make the dressing, use a mortar and pestle to pound the garlic into a rough paste. Work in the sugar, fish sauce, lime juice and chilli flakes, pounding until the sugar dissolves. Alternatively, chop the ingredients into a paste using a small food processor.

Combine the sliced chicken with the salad ingredients and the reserved tablespoon of poaching liquid. Add the dressing and toss until well combined. Gently toss in the quail eggs. Sprinkle with ground roasted peanuts and fried shallots.

This is a fantastic dish to share with friends over a few beers. Pile the mussels into a huge bowl in the middle of the table and have everyone help themselves.

Mussels with chilli and basil

1 kg (2 lb 4 oz) mussels
2 tablespoons vegetable oil
375 ml (1¹/2 cups) chicken stock* or water
1–2 teaspoons fish sauce
2 tablespoons chilli jam*
2 handfuls Thai basil leaves

Paste
3 garlic cloves, peeled
2 long red chillies, chopped

To serve
1 handful coriander (cilantro) leaves

Serves 6

Wash the mussels well, scrubbing the shells and pulling off the hairy beards. Discard any mussels that are open and do not close when tapped sharply on the work surface.

To make the paste, use a mortar and pestle to pound the garlic, chillies and ¹/2 teaspoon salt into a paste. Alternatively, chop the ingredients into a paste using a small food processor.

Heat a wok over high heat. Add the oil and heat until hot. Add the chilli–garlic paste and fry for 1 minute, or until fragrant, then add the stock and mussels. Cover the wok and steam the mussels for about 2 minutes, or until just opened. Discard any that have not opened by this time. Stir in the fish sauce and chilli jam and cook for 1 minute, then add the basil leaves. Remove from the heat.

To serve, scoop the mussels and sauce into a bowl and sprinkle with the coriander leaves.

These dumplings were one of my favourite snacks as a child. My mother would serve them mid-afternoon or after dinner. Now I like to eat them as a starter before the main meal.

Steamed prawn and vegetable dumplings with black vinegar

1 packet won ton skins (you'll need about 16)

Filling
3 dried shiitake mushrooms
300 g (10^1/$_2$ oz) raw small prawns (shrimp), peeled and deveined
3 tablespoons roughly chopped Chinese celery
1^1/$_2$ spring onions (scallions), finely sliced
1 tablespoon cornflour (cornstarch)
2 teaspoons oyster sauce
^{1}/$_4$ teaspoon finely grated fresh ginger
^{1}/$_4$ teaspoon sesame oil

To serve
3 tablespoons black vinegar
2 tablespoons coriander (cilantro) leaves, roughly chopped

Makes about 16

To make the filling, soak the mushrooms in hot water for 30 minutes, then drain. Discard the stem and finely slice the caps. Put the prawns into a food processor and process briefly until roughly minced (ground). Transfer to a large bowl and add the rest of the filling, ^{1}/$_2$ teaspoon salt and a pinch of white pepper. Mix until well combined. Use your hand to lift up the prawn mixture and then slap it back into the bowl a few times—this will give the filling a firmer texture.

Lay a won ton skin on a flat surface. Put about 1 tablespoon of filling in the middle of the skin. Lift all the corners up, leaving the top of the filling exposed. Repeat until all the filling is used up.

Bring a wok or large saucepan of water to the boil. Put the dumplings in a steamer lined with banana leaves or baking paper—you may need to do this in batches. Sit the steamer over the wok of boiling water, making sure the base of the steamer does not touch the water. Put the lid on the steamer and cook the dumplings for 6–7 minutes.

Serve the dumplings accompanied with a small bowl of black vinegar for guests to dip their dumplings into. Alternatively, pour a little of the black vinegar over the dumplings, sprinkle with coriander leaves, then serve.

To appreciate the mild, sweet flavour of the scallops, keep the topping simple.

Steamed scallops with ginger and spring onions

16 scallops on their shells
2 teaspoons finely grated fresh ginger

Sauce
4 tablespoons Shaoxing rice wine
1 tablespoon light soy sauce
1/2 teaspoon sesame oil
1 teaspoon sugar

To serve
4–5 spring onions (scallions),
finely julienned
3 tablespoons vegetable oil
1 handful coriander (cilantro) leaves

Serves 4

Remove the scallops from their shells. Slice the small, hard white muscle off the side of each scallop and pull off any membrane, leaving the roes intact. Clean the shells, then return each scallop to its shell.

To make the sauce, combine the rice wine, soy sauce, sesame oil, sugar and a pinch of white pepper in a bowl. Stir thoroughly until the sugar dissolves.

Bring a wok or large saucepan of water to the boil. Put the scallops on a heatproof plate that fits in a steamer—you may need to do this in two batches. Top each scallop with a small amount of ginger and 1 teaspoon of the sauce. Sit the steamer over the wok of boiling water, making sure the base of the steamer does not touch the water. Put the lid on the steamer and steam the scallops for 3–4 minutes, or until cooked.

To serve, remove the scallops from the steamer and lift onto a serving dish. Drizzle with the remaining sauce and sprinkle with spring onion. Heat the oil in a saucepan until smoky, then carefully drizzle over the scallops. Garnish with coriander leaves.

These pancakes are a twist on the classic Peking duck pancake, but use lamb instead of duck. Lamb is not a feature of most Asian cuisines, but I love it and am always experimenting with new ways to use it.

Lamb fillet pancakes with hoisin sauce

300 g (10^1/$_2$ oz) lamb loin fillet or backstrap, trimmed
1 packet Mandarin (Peking duck) pancakes (you'll need about 12)
2 small Lebanese (short) cucumbers, deseeded and roughly julienned into 8 cm (3 inch) lengths
4 spring onions (scallions), julienned into 8 cm (3 inch) lengths
10–12 coriander (cilantro) sprigs
3 tablespoons hoisin sauce

Marinade
2 garlic cloves, peeled
1 lemon grass stem (white part only), chopped
2 tablespoons vegetable oil
1 teaspoon sesame oil

Makes 10–12

To make the marinade, use a mortar and pestle to pound the garlic, lemon grass and a pinch of salt together. Add both the vegetable and sesame oils and stir until well combined. Alternatively, chop the ingredients into a paste using a small food processor. Scoop the marinade into a non-metallic bowl with the lamb fillet. Coat the lamb well, then marinate in the refrigerator for 3–4 hours, or overnight if time permits.

Remove the lamb from the marinade and roughly pat dry. Preheat a chargrill pan or barbecue hotplate over medium–high heat. Cook the lamb fillet for 2–3 minutes on each side, or to your liking. Rest for 5 minutes before slicing into 8 cm (3 inch) lengths on the diagonal.

Bring a wok or large saucepan of water to the boil. Put the pancakes in a steamer lined with banana leaves or baking paper—you may need to do this in two batches. Sit the steamer over the wok, making sure the base of the steamer does not touch the water. Put the lid on the steamer and steam the pancakes for 2–3 minutes, or until cooked through. Alternatively, warm them for 30 seconds in a microwave.

To serve, lay out a pancake and put 1–2 slices of lamb in the centre. Top with cucumber, spring onion and coriander and drizzle with the hoisin sauce. Roll up and serve.

Two cultures meet on the one plate—Vietnamese-style stuffed squid with Malaysian-style tomato sambal.

Vietnamese stuffed squid with tomato sambal

6 small–medium squid
2 tablespoons vegetable oil

Stuffing
3 large fresh or dried cloud ear fungus
25 g (1 oz) bean thread vermicelli
200 g (7 oz) minced (ground) pork
3 spring onions (scallions), finely sliced
1 garlic clove, finely sliced
pinch of five-spice powder

Tomato sambal
1 tablespoon vegetable oil
1/2 onion, diced
2 garlic cloves, crushed
1/2 long red chilli, chopped
3 tomatoes, diced
3 tablespoons tomato sauce (ketchup)
2 spring onions (scallions), sliced

To serve
6 coriander (cilantro) sprigs

Serves 6

To clean the squid, firmly pull the head and innards from the body. Wash the body well. Cut the head off just below the eyes, leaving the tentacles intact. Pull the transparent quill out of the body and rinse out the tube. Peel off the outer membrane. Keep the tentacles for stuffing and finely chop them.

If you are using fresh cloud ear fungus, finely chop them. If using dried, first soak them in hot water for 20 minutes, then drain and finely chop. Soak the bean thread vermicelli in cold water for 10 minutes, or until soft. Drain and cut into 2.5 cm (1 inch) lengths.

Combine all the stuffing ingredients and a pinch of salt and pepper in a bowl. Mix in the reserved chopped squid tentacles. Stuff the mixture into the squid bodies, leaving some room for the filling to expand during cooking. Close the end of each squid body with a toothpick.

To make the tomato sambal, heat the oil in a saucepan and fry the onion and garlic for a few minutes, or until softened. Add the chilli and cook for 1 minute, then add the tomato and cook until the tomato starts to break up. Add the tomato sauce, spring onion and a pinch of salt and cook for a further 1 minute. Remove from the heat.

To cook the squid, heat the oil in a non-stick frying pan. Fry the stuffed squid, turning frequently until they are browned, then cover and reduce the heat. Cook for a further 10–15 minutes, or until cooked through. Remove and drain on paper towels.

To serve, remove the toothpicks from the squid. Carefully slice and put one squid onto each plate. Season with some white pepper. Serve the tomato sambal sauce on the side and garnish with coriander sprigs.

This dish was inspired by the blend of fresh herbs and tender beef that is the basis of Thai beef salad.

Chargrilled beef with chilli jam and green papaya salad

4 x 125 g (4¹/₂ oz) beef rump steaks or
sirloin steaks, trimmed
1 tablespoon peanut oil

Dressing
2 garlic cloves, peeled
1 long red chilli, deseeded and chopped
1¹/₂ tablespoons shaved palm sugar
3 tablespoons lime juice
2 tablespoons fish sauce

Salad
¹/₂ green papaya, peeled, deseeded
and finely julienned
4 cherry tomatoes, quartered
1 small handful mint leaves
1 small handful Thai basil leaves
1 small handful coriander (cilantro) leaves

To serve
4 x 12 cm (5 inch) square pieces of
banana leaf
1¹/₂ tablespoons chilli jam*
2 tablespoons ground roasted peanuts*

Serves 4

Heat a chargrill pan or barbecue hotplate over medium–high heat. Add the oil, then cook the beef for 2–3 minutes on each side, or until cooked to medium. Rest for 5 minutes, then slice thinly.

To make the dressing, use a mortar and pestle to pound the garlic and chilli together. Work in the sugar, lime juice and fish sauce, pounding until the sugar dissolves. Alternatively, chop the ingredients using a small food processor. Put all the salad ingredients in a large bowl, add the dressing and toss well.

To serve, put a piece of banana leaf in the centre of each plate. Top with the sliced beef and a heaped teaspoon of chilli jam. Make a neat pile of the salad on the side, then sprinkle with ground peanuts.

Fresh lotus stem is crunchier and has a fresher flavour than the packaged variety, but if fresh is not available, you can buy jars of lotus stems in brine at most Asian grocery stores.

Young lotus stem salad with prawns

Salad
150 g (5¹/2 oz) young lotus stem, cut into 10 cm (4 inch) lengths
16 cooked prawns (shrimp), peeled, deveined and halved lengthways
4 red Asian shallots, sliced
1 long red chilli, finely julienned
1 large handful Vietnamese mint leaves
1 handful coriander (cilantro) leaves
large pinch of sugar
1 teaspoon fish sauce
1 tablespoon lime juice
3 tablespoons nuoc cham (Vietnamese dipping sauce)*

To serve
2 tablespoons coarsely ground roasted peanuts*
2 tablespoons fried shallots*

Serves 4

If you are using lotus stem in brine, drain it, then soak in 125 ml (¹/2 cup) water, 1 tablespoon vinegar and 1 tablespoon sugar for 15 minutes. Drain again, then cut into 10 cm (4 inch) lengths. If you are using fresh lotus stem, simply cut it into 10 cm (4 inch) lengths.

Put all the salad ingredients in a large bowl and toss together well. This salad should taste sour, sweet, and a little bit salty.

To serve, divide the salad among four serving bowls, then sprinkle with peanuts and fried shallots.

For the greatest visual impact, slice the rolls in half on the diagonal so you can see the different layers of colour.

Prawn rice paper rolls

Filling
60 g (2¹/₄ oz) dried rice vermicelli
8 rice paper wrappers
8 medium butter lettuce leaves
8 cooked prawns (shrimp), peeled and deveined, then sliced in half lengthways
1 small handful large mint leaves
1 small carrot, finely julienned
1 cucumber, peeled and julienned
1 handful coriander (cilantro) leaves

Dipping sauce
4 tablespoons hoisin sauce
1 tablespoon rice vinegar
1 tablespoon sugar

To serve
1 tablespoon ground roasted peanuts*

Serves 4

Put the vermicelli in a bowl and cover with boiling water. Leave to soften for 5–7 minutes. Drain, refresh under cold water, then drain once more.

Fill a large bowl with hot water. Taking one rice paper wrapper at a time, dip them into the water for about 15 seconds, or until soft, then lay out flat on a clean damp tea towel. Lay a lettuce leaf over each one. Put two pieces of prawn horizontally across the middle of each leaf. Top with two or three mint leaves, a little carrot, cucumber, coriander and rice vermicelli. Fold the bottom of the wrapper up over the filling, then fold the two sides in. Roll up as tightly as possible with your hands. Keep each roll under a damp cloth. Repeat with the rest of the wrappers and filling.

To make the dipping sauce, combine all the ingredients and 2 tablespoons water, stirring until the sugar dissolves. Transfer to a small serving dish.

To serve, arrange two rice paper rolls in a crisscross pattern on each plate. Sprinkle the peanuts onto the sauce and serve in a small bowl.

The quails are marinated in traditional Chinese flavourings—ginger, rice wine and five-spice powder—with a hint of Southeast Asia coming through in the fish sauce.

Twice-cooked quails with pepper and salt mix

4 large quails
vegetable oil, for deep-frying
1 quantity pepper and salt mix*

Marinade
2 garlic cloves, peeled
1/2 teaspoon finely grated fresh ginger
1 teaspoon sugar
1 tablespoon fish sauce
2 tablespoons Shaoxing rice wine
1/2 teaspoon five-spice powder

To serve
4 x 12 cm (5 inch) square pieces
of banana leaf
4 lime wedges

Serves 4

Cut each quail along the backbone, then turn over and push down on the breastbone to flatten. Cut along the breastbone to cut the quails into two halves. Clean and dry.

To make the marinade, use a mortar and pestle to pound the garlic and ginger together. Mix in the rest of the ingredients and a pinch of salt and white pepper. Alternatively, chop the ingredients into a paste using a small food processor. Scoop the marinade into a non-metallic bowl with the quails. Turn to coat the quails well, then marinate in the fridge for 3–4 hours. Remove the quails from the marinade.

Bring a wok or large saucepan of water to the boil. Put the quails, breast-side up, in a steamer lined with banana leaves or baking paper—you may need to do this in batches. Sit the steamer over the wok of boiling water, making sure the base of the steamer does not touch the water. Put the lid on the steamer and steam for 3 minutes, or until just cooked. Remove from the steamer. Leave to cool, then refrigerate for 2 hours.

Fill a wok or deep-fat fryer one-third full of oil and heat to 170–180°C (325–350°F), or until a cube of bread dropped into the oil browns in 15–20 seconds. Deep-fry two pieces of the quail at a time for 2–3 minutes, or until lightly browned and cooked. Keep warm in a low oven while you cook the rest.

To serve, put a piece of banana leaf in the centre of each plate, then top with two quail halves. Sprinkle with the pepper and salt mix and serve with a lime wedge on the side.

In China, this dish would normally be served using barbecued pork from a barbecued meat shop. But for moister, more flavoursome meat, braise the pork in a stock infused with five-spice powder and star anise.

Braised five-spice pork fillet with bean sprout salad

400 g (14 oz) pork neck fillet
4 tablespoons hoisin dressing*

Braising stock
2 garlic cloves, crushed
5 cm (2 inch) knob of fresh ginger, crushed
2 teaspoons five-spice powder
6 star anise
2 tablespoons soy sauce
1 tablespoon sugar
1 teaspoon salt

Salad
100 g (1 cup) bean sprouts, trimmed
50 g (1³/4 oz) Chinese cabbage, finely sliced
1 celery stalk, finely sliced on the diagonal
1 handful mint leaves
1 handful coriander (cilantro) leaves
2 long red chillies, deseeded and finely julienned
3 spring onions (scallions), finely julienned
1 tablespoon finely sliced fresh young ginger

To serve
1–1¹/2 tablespoons roasted sesame seeds*
2 tablespoons fried shallots* (optional)

Serves 4

Combine all the braising stock ingredients in a large saucepan. Add the pork and top with enough water to cover the pork fillet. Bring to the boil, then reduce the heat and simmer for 5–7 minutes. Remove the pan from the heat, cover with a tight lid and allow the pork to completely cool in the stock.

To make the salad, put all the salad ingredients in a large bowl and toss together.

To serve, slice the pork fillet into 2.5 mm (¹/8 inch) slices on the diagonal. Divide the salad among four plates, then top with the pork. Drizzle with the hoisin dressing, then sprinkle with sesame seeds and, if you wish, fried shallots.

I love fresh coriander noodles both for their flavour and unusual colour. They can be hard to find, but many shops sell fresh spinach noodles that you can use in their place.

Roasted duck and coriander noodle salad

1 Chinese roasted duck, boned and sliced

Dressing
3 tablespoons light soy sauce
2 tablespoons black vinegar
1 tablespoon shaved palm sugar
1/4 teaspoon sesame oil
1 tablespoon mirin (optional)

Salad
200 g (7 oz) fresh coriander (cilantro) noodles or other green noodles
1 handful mint leaves
1 handful coriander (cilantro) leaves
2 spring onions (scallions), finely julienned
3 red Asian shallots, sliced

To serve
1 tablespoon roasted shredded coconut*
1 tablespoon roasted sesame seeds*

Serves 4

To make the dressing, combine all the dressing ingredients and stir until the sugar dissolves.

Blanch the coriander noodles in boiling water for 1 minute, then refresh under cold water. Combine with the remaining salad ingredients and moisten with the dressing.

To serve, arrange the salad in a bowl, then top with slices of duck and a sprinkling of roasted shredded coconut and sesame seeds.

This salad epitomizes everything I love best about food—vibrant colours, contrasting textures and fresh flavours.

Chargrilled baby octopus with green papaya salad

16 baby octopus (ask your fishmonger to clean them for you)
1 quantity green papaya salad and dressing (see page 43)

Marinade
2 garlic cloves, peeled
1 long red chilli, deseeded and chopped
2 lemon grass stems (white part only), finely sliced
3 tablespoons vegetable oil

To serve (optional)
2 tablespoons ground roasted peanuts*
4 lime wedges

Serves 4

If you haven't been able to buy cleaned octopus, do it yourself. Cut between the head and tentacles, just below the eyes. Remove the beak by pushing it out through the centre of the tentacles. Cut the eyes from the head by slicing off a small round. Remove the intestines by pushing them out of the head.

To make the marinade, use a mortar and pestle to pound the garlic, chilli and lemon grass to a coarse paste. Stir in the oil. Alternatively, chop the ingredients into a paste using a small food processor. Scoop the marinade into a non-metallic bowl with the octopus. Coat the octopus well, then marinate in the refrigerator for 1–2 hours.

Remove the octopus from the marinade. Preheat a chargrill pan or barbecue hotplate over high heat and cook the octopus for 3–4 minutes, or until cooked.

To serve, toss the green papaya salad with its dressing, then divide it among four plates. Top with the octopus and sprinkle with peanuts, if using. Serve with a lime wedge, if desired.

Pre-cooked prawns are not only easy to use, but also have a fresh, salty tang from being cooked in sea water.

Vietnamese chicken and prawn salad

200 g (7 oz) chicken breast fillet
12 cooked prawns (shrimp), peeled, deveined and halved lengthways

Dressing
1 long red chilli, deseeded and chopped
1/2 garlic clove
3 teaspoons shaved palm sugar
1 1/2 tablespoons lime juice
2 tablespoons fish sauce
2 teaspoons rice vinegar

Salad
100 g (1 1/3 cups) finely shredded white cabbage
1 small carrot, finely julienned
1 Lebanese (short) cucumber, deseeded and julienned
1 large handful Vietnamese mint leaves
1 handful coriander (cilantro) leaves
1 long red chilli, deseeded and julienned

To serve
2 tablespoons ground roasted peanuts*
2 tablespoons fried shallots*
4 lime wedges

Serves 4

Heat 2 litres (8 cups) water in a small saucepan. Add the chicken fillet and gently simmer for 5–6 minutes, or until cooked. Take the pan off the heat, cover with a lid and allow the chicken to cool in the water. Remove from the water, pat dry, then slice.

To make the dressing, use a mortar and pestle to pound the chilli and garlic together. Work in the palm sugar and lime juice, then the fish sauce, vinegar and 1 1/2 tablespoons water, pounding until the sugar dissolves. Alternatively, chop the ingredients into a paste using a small food processor.

To make the salad, combine all the ingredients in a bowl and toss together. Add the sliced chicken and prawns, drizzle with the dressing, then gently toss together.

To serve, divide the salad among four plates and sprinkle with ground roasted peanuts and fried shallots. Serve with a lime wedge.

These fresh oysters are served with a spicy Asian version of classic basil pesto.

Fresh oysters with chilli, coriander and basil pesto

24 oysters, freshly shucked

Pesto
1/2 garlic clove
1 red Asian shallot, sliced
1/4 long red chilli, chopped
1 spring onion (scallion), chopped
1 tablespoon chopped roasted peanuts*
12 Thai basil leaves
2 coriander (cilantro) stems with leaves
pinch of sugar
2 teaspoons lime juice
1/4 teaspoon fish sauce
2 1/2 tablespoons peanut oil

To serve
2 finely julienned deseeded red chillies

Serves 4–6

To make the pesto, use a mortar and pestle to pound all the pesto ingredients, except the oil, into a coarse paste. Slowly pour in the oil, stirring constantly until the pesto has reached the consistency of a thick paste. Alternatively, combine all the pesto ingredients, except the oil, in a food processor and process until coarsely chopped. With the motor on, add the oil in a thin, steady stream, until a thick paste forms.

To serve, spoon 1/2 teaspoon pesto onto each oyster and garnish with julienned chilli.

Fresh galangal has a distinctive red–gold skin. Galangal is also available sliced and dried but as with anything, fresh is best.

Mussels with chilli and galangal

1 kg (2 lb 4 oz) mussels
375 ml (1¹/₂ cups) chicken stock* or water
2 lemon grass stems, bruised
14 slices of fresh galangal
6 makrut (kaffir) lime leaves, torn
1 large tomato, cut into wedges
2 long red chillies, deseeded and sliced lengthways
3 tablespoons tamarind water*
2 tablespoons fish sauce
2 teaspoons sugar

To serve
1 handful bean sprouts, trimmed
1 large handful Vietnamese mint leaves

Serves 6

Wash the mussels well, scrubbing the shells and pulling off the hairy beards. Discard any mussels that are open and do not close when tapped sharply on the work surface.

Bring the stock or water to the boil in a wok. Add the lemon grass, galangal, lime leaves, tomato and chillies and simmer for 2–3 minutes. Add the mussels and cover the wok with a lid. Simmer for about 2 minutes, or until the mussels just open, discarding any that have not opened by this time. Stir in the tamarind water, fish sauce and sugar, then taste—the liquid should taste sour, sweet, and a little bit salty.

To serve, transfer the mussels and cooking liquid to a bowl. Garnish with bean sprouts and Vietnamese mint leaves.

These are a party speciality—they are full of flavour, can be made in advance and need only the briefest flash in the oil just before you serve them.

Chicken won tons with plum sauce

1 packet won ton skins (you'll need about 20)
vegetable oil, for deep-frying

Filling
100 g (3 1/2 oz) minced (ground) chicken
1/2 teaspoon finely grated fresh ginger
1 small garlic clove, crushed
2 spring onions (scallions), finely sliced
6 coriander (cilantro) stems with leaves, finely sliced
1 teaspoon oyster sauce

To serve
plum sauce

Makes 20

To make the filling, put the chicken mince in a food processor with the rest of the filling ingredients and a pinch of salt and white pepper. Process until the mixture becomes smooth.

Lay the won ton skins on a flat surface. Place 1 teaspoon of chicken mixture in the centre of each won ton skin. Run a wet finger around the edge of the wrapper and then fold it in half to form a triangle. Seal the edges, then bring the two outside corners of the triangle together and pinch them so they stick together. Repeat with the rest of the filling and won ton skins.

Fill a wok or deep-fat fryer one-half full of oil and heat to 160–170°C (315–325°F), or until a cube of bread dropped into the oil browns in 20–35 seconds. Working in small batches, drop won tons into the oil and fry for 1 minute, or until golden brown and cooked. Remove and drain on paper towels.

Serve the won tons on a plate with the plum sauce.

These easy-to-make rolls are a robust and substantial variation of the classic spring roll. When cut open, they release an intoxicating lemon grass aroma.

Crispy lemon grass beef rolls

8 spring roll wrappers
2 egg whites, lightly beaten
vegetable oil, for deep-frying

Filling
30 g (1 oz) bean thread vermicelli
2 tablespoons vegetable oil
1/2 onion, sliced
1 garlic clove, crushed
300 g (10 1/2 oz) beef rump or sirloin, finely sliced into strips
2 lemon grass stems (white part only), finely sliced and chopped
2 tablespoons oyster sauce
4 spring onions (scallions), finely sliced
large pinch of five-spice powder

To serve
sweet chilli sauce*
4 coriander (cilantro) sprigs

Makes 4

To make the filling, soak the bean thread vermicelli in cold water for 10 minutes. Drain and cut into 3 cm (1 1/4 inch) lengths. Heat the oil in a hot wok. Add the onion and garlic and stir-fry for 2–3 minutes, or until soft, but not browned. Add the beef, lemon grass and oyster sauce and stir-fry for a further 2–3 minutes, or until the beef is medium–well done. Add the lengths of vermicelli and mix well. Remove the wok from the heat and leave to cool.

Add the spring onions, five-spice powder and a pinch of salt and white pepper to the beef mixture and mix well.

Put two spring roll wrappers on a work surface, one on top of the other so they form a double layer. Place one-quarter of the beef mixture in a sausage shape across one corner of each double spring roll wrapper. Brush the edges of the wrapper with beaten egg whites and roll up tightly, folding in the sides as you roll so the filling is completely enclosed.

Fill a wok or deep-fat fryer one-third full of oil and heat to 170°C (325°F), or until a cube of bread dropped into the oil browns in 20 seconds. Drop the spring rolls into the oil and deep-fry for 2–3 minutes, or until golden brown and cooked. Remove and drain on paper towels.

To serve, cut each roll on the diagonal with a sharp knife. Serve with sweet chilli sauce and a sprig of coriander.

The secret to keeping the quail moist and flavoursome is to regularly baste it with the marinade while cooking.

Chargrilled spicy quail with watercress salad

4 large quails

Marinade
2 garlic cloves, peeled
6 coriander (cilantro) roots, cleaned and chopped
2 tablespoons chilli bean sauce
2 tablespoons Shaoxing rice wine
2 tablespoons vegetable oil
1 tablespoon light soy sauce
1 teaspoon sugar
1/2 teaspoon finely grated fresh ginger
pinch of five-spice powder

Salad
25 g (2 handfuls) watercress sprigs
1 quantity black vinegar dressing*

Serves 4

Cut each quail along the backbone, then turn over and push down on the breastbone to flatten. Cut along the breastbone to cut the quails into two halves. Clean and dry.

To make the marinade, use a mortar and pestle to pound the garlic and coriander roots together. Work in the chilli bean sauce, rice wine, oil, soy sauce, sugar, ginger and five-spice powder, pounding until the sugar dissolves. Alternatively, chop the ingredients into a paste using a small food processor. Scoop the marinade into a non-metallic bowl with the quails. Turn to coat the quails well, then marinate in the refrigerator for 6 hours, or overnight if time permits.

Preheat a chargrill pan or barbecue hotplate over high heat. Remove the quails from the marinade, reserving the marinade. Cook the quails for 4 minutes on each side, basting occasionally with the reserved marinade and pressing down firmly with a spatula.

To serve, moisten the watercress with the black vinegar dressing—you may not need it all. Divide the salad among four plates, then put two quail halves on each plate.

In Vietnam, sweet potato is as ubiquitous as potato is in the West. I've mixed it with prawns to make these delicious fritters.

Fried sweet potato and prawn fritters with tomato sambal

90 g (1/2 cup) rice flour
100 g (3 1/2 oz) sweet potato, peeled and grated
6 egg whites
12 raw king prawns (shrimp), peeled, deveined and cut in half
vegetable oil, for deep-frying

To serve
4 x 12 cm (5 inch) square pieces of banana leaf
1 quantity tomato sambal (see page 40)

Serves 4

Combine the flour, grated sweet potato, egg whites and prawns in a large bowl. Fill a wok or deep-fat fryer one-half full of oil and heat to 180°C (350°F), or until a cube of bread dropped into the oil browns in 15 seconds. Deep-fry heaped tablespoonfuls of the prawn batter for 2–3 minutes, or until golden and crisp. Drain on paper towels.

To serve, put a banana leaf on a serving plate. Arrange the prawn fritters on top and serve with tomato sambal.

second

second

I love the Asian tradition of the banquet—a table laden with many different dishes and bowls of steaming rice, with everyone trying a little of everything. With the busy lives most people lead it's hard to imagine eating like that every day, so I've designed the recipes in this chapter so they can be used either as part of an Asian feast or as a stand-alone main meal.

You'll notice that most recipes serve two to four people. What this means is that if you want to pick one meal with no accompaniments, it will serve two people. But if you're offering a selection of other dishes, it will serve four people. In general, for a banquet of four people, pick one vegetarian meal, then two other mains. If you're serving six people, pick three seafood or meat dishes and one vegetarian meal. All you need to add is a heaped bowl of freshly steamed rice.

When choosing what to serve, let the season guide you. Pick heavier curries or braised dishes for winter and lighter salads or seafood dishes for summer. If you're looking for a suitable wine to serve with spicy food, pick a good fruity wine, such as a sauvignon blanc, pinot gris, verdelho or gewürztraminer.

Ginger and spring onion sauce is a traditional Chinese accompaniment for fish. Though I've used barramundi, you can use snapper, cod or any other firm white fish fillets.

Steamed barramundi fillets with ginger and spring onion sauce

4 x 200 g (7 oz) barramundi fillets
300 g (10½ oz) bok choy (pak choi), cut into quarters lengthways

Sauce
3 tablespoons peanut oil
1 garlic clove, crushed
3 tablespoons light soy sauce
4 tablespoons chicken stock* or water
3 tablespoons Shaoxing rice wine
1 tablespoon oyster sauce
3 tablespoons julienned fresh ginger
12 x 6 cm (2½ inch) pieces of spring onion (scallion), using mainly the white part
2 teaspoons sugar
¼ teaspoon sesame oil

To serve
1 handful finely julienned spring onion (scallion), green part only
1 handful coriander (cilantro) leaves
1 long red chilli, deseeded and julienned

Serves 4

Bring a wok or large saucepan of water to the boil. Pat the fish dry with paper towels, then season with a pinch of salt and white pepper. Put the fillets in a steamer lined with banana leaves or baking paper—you may need to do this in batches. Sit the steamer over the wok, making sure the base of the steamer does not touch the water. Put the lid on the steamer and steam the fish for 7–9 minutes, depending on the thickness of the fish. The fish is ready when the flesh flakes easily when tested with a fork.

To make the ginger and spring onion sauce, heat the oil in a saucepan. Add the garlic and fry it briefly (20–30 seconds) until it becomes fragrant but not browned, then add the rest of the ingredients and a pinch of white pepper. Reduce the heat and simmer for about 2 minutes.

Blanch the bok choy in boiling water for 30 seconds. Drain well.

To serve, divide the bok choy among four plates. Carefully lift a fish fillet onto the bok choy. Pour the sauce over the fish. Garnish with the spring onion, coriander and chilli.

Before you deep-fry basil leaves, make sure they are bone dry. Even the tiniest amount of water on the leaves will make the oil splatter and hiss.

Wok-fried Vietnamese turmeric chicken with coconut milk and asparagus

500 g (1 lb 2 oz) chicken breast fillet, sliced
2 garlic cloves, finely diced
1 onion, roughly sliced
2 large lemon grass stems (white part only), finely sliced
1 long red chilli, sliced on the diagonal
3 tablespoons peanut oil
500 ml (2 cups) coconut milk
300 g (2 bunches) asparagus, trimmed and sliced on the diagonal
1 1/2 tablespoons fish sauce
1 tablespoon oyster sauce
5 teaspoons sugar
2 teaspoons ground turmeric

To serve
vegetable oil, for deep-frying
1 handful Thai basil leaves
4 tablespoons roughly chopped roasted peanuts* (optional)

Serves 4–6

Combine the chicken, garlic, onion, lemon grass and chilli in a bowl and mix well. Heat the oil in a hot wok. Add the chicken in batches and stir-fry each batch for 1–2 minutes, or until cooked. Remove from the wok. Return all the chicken to the wok. Pour in the coconut milk, then add the asparagus and bring to the boil. Reduce the heat and simmer for 1 minute. Add the fish sauce, oyster sauce, sugar, turmeric and a pinch of salt and stir-fry for 2 minutes, or until the asparagus is tender.

Fill a wok or heavy-based saucepan one-third full of oil and heat to 180°C (350°F), or until a cube of bread dropped into the oil browns in 15 seconds. Add the basil and fry briefly until crisp—be very careful as the oil is very hot and may spit at you. Drain on crumpled paper towels.

To serve, divide the chicken among four plates, then sprinkle with the fried basil and, if you like, peanuts.

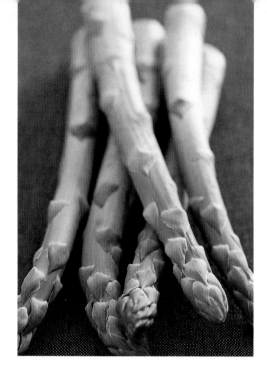

This makes a filling, delicious vegetarian main meal but it is equally good as a side dish served with curries.

Stir-fried asparagus, mushroom and cloud ear fungus

4–6 dried shiitake mushrooms
10 g (1/4 oz) fresh or dried cloud ear fungus
2 tablespoons vegetable oil
2 garlic cloves, crushed
150 g (1 bunch) asparagus, trimmed and sliced on the diagonal into 5 cm (2 inch) pieces
6 large oyster mushrooms, roughly torn
3 tablespoons chicken stock*
2 tablespoons Shaoxing rice wine
1 tablespoon light soy sauce
1 tablespoon dark soy sauce
1/2 teaspoon sugar

Serves 2–4

Soak the shiitake mushrooms in hot water for 30 minutes, then drain. Discard the stems and cut the caps in half. If you are using fresh cloud ear fungus, finely chop them. If using dried, first soak them in hot water for 20 minutes, then drain and finely chop, if necessary.

Heat the oil in a hot wok. Add the garlic and stir-fry briefly (20–30 seconds) until fragrant. Add the asparagus and shiitake mushrooms and stir-fry for 1 minute. Add the oyster mushrooms, cloud ear fungus, stock, rice wine, soy sauces and sugar and cook for 2 minutes. Serve immediately.

Most Asian countries have a thriving food industry centred around street vendors, who specialize in assembling noodle dishes or salads such as this one on demand.

Chargrilled lemon grass chicken with rice vermicelli salad

300 g (10^{1}/$_{2}$ oz) chicken thigh fillet
1 tablespoon vegetable oil

Marinade
2 lemon grass stems (white part only), chopped
2 garlic cloves, peeled
4 white peppercorns
^{1}/$_{2}$ teaspoon sugar
1 teaspoon fish sauce
2 tablespoons vegetable oil

Salad
100 g (3^{1}/$_{2}$ oz) dried rice vermicelli
90 g (1 cup) bean sprouts, trimmed
1 small handful mint leaves, sliced
1 small handful Thai basil leaves, sliced
1 small handful coriander (cilantro) leaves
^{1}/$_{2}$ Lebanese (short) cucumber, deseeded and julienned
5–6 tablespoons nuoc cham (Vietnamese dipping sauce)*

Spring onion oil
1 tablespoon vegetable oil
2 spring onions (scallions), finely sliced

To serve
2 tablespoons ground roasted peanuts*
lime wedges

Serves 2–4

To make the marinade, use a mortar and pestle to pound the lemon grass, garlic, peppercorns and a pinch of salt into a paste. Work in the sugar, fish sauce and oil, pounding until the sugar dissolves. Alternatively, chop the ingredients into a paste using a small food processor. Scoop the marinade into a non-metallic bowl with the chicken. Coat the chicken in the marinade, then marinate in the refrigerator overnight.

To make the salad, put the rice vermicelli in a bowl and cover with boiling water. Leave to soften for 5–7 minutes. Drain, refresh under cold water, then drain again. Transfer to a large bowl, add the remaining salad ingredients and mix well.

To make the spring onion oil, heat the oil until hot, then add the spring onions and a pinch of salt and cook for 30 seconds. Take the pan off the heat and set aside.

Preheat a chargrill pan or barbecue hotplate over medium–high heat. Heat 1 tablespoon vegetable oil in the pan. Remove the chicken from the marinade and cook it for 7 minutes on each side, or until cooked, occasionally firmly pressing down on the chicken with a spatula. Remove from the pan, rest in a warm place for 5 minutes, then slice.

To serve, pile the salad into a serving bowl and top with the chicken slices. Sprinkle with ground peanuts and drizzle with the spring onion oil. Serve with lime wedges.

Hokkien noodles are among the thickest and most satisfying of all noodles.

Malaysian-style stir-fried egg noodles with prawns and squid

2 squid tubes
200 g (7 oz) hokkien (egg) noodles
3 tablespoons vegetable oil
4 king prawns (shrimp), peeled and deveined, tails intact
100 g (3^{1}/$_{2}$ oz) choy sum, cut into 5 cm (2 inch) lengths
3 tablespoons chicken stock*
1 tablespoon oyster sauce
1 tablespoon dark soy sauce
45 g (^{1}/$_{2}$ cup) bean sprouts, trimmed

Paste
2 dried long red chillies
1 garlic clove
2 red Asian shallots

To serve
1 handful coriander (cilantro) leaves
lime wedges

Serves 2–4

Open up the squid tubes and scrub off any soft jelly-like substance, then score the inside of the flesh with a fine crisscross pattern, making sure you do not cut all the way through. Cut the squid into 1 x 2 cm (^{1}/$_{2}$ x ^{3}/$_{4}$ inch) pieces. Run the noodles under warm water to separate them, then drain.

To make the paste, soak the chillies in hot water for 1–2 minutes, then drain. Remove the stems and seeds, then roughly chop. Use a mortar and pestle to pound the chillies, garlic, shallots and a pinch of salt into a paste. Alternatively, chop the ingredients into a paste using a small food processor.

Heat the oil in a hot wok and fry the paste until fragrant. Add the prawns and squid pieces and stir-fry for 2 minutes, or until the prawns and squid are nearly cooked. Be careful not to overcook the squid as it will become tough. Toss in the noodles and choy sum and stir-fry for 2 minutes. Add the stock, oyster sauce, dark soy sauce and bean sprouts and stir-fry for another 1 minute.

To serve, pile the noodles onto a plate or bowl. Garnish with coriander leaves and lime wedges.

Dried beancurd sticks are similar to beancurd skins, but thicker. Like lily buds and cloud ear fungus, they would be found in many kitchen cupboards throughout Asia; elsewhere you may need to source them from a specialist Asian food shop.

Braised vegetables

20 dried lily buds
8 small dried shiitake mushrooms
30 g (1 oz) dried cloud ear fungus
40 g (1^1/$_2$ oz) dried beancurd sticks, broken into 5 cm (2 inch) lengths
3 tablespoons vegetable oil
2 garlic cloves, crushed
1 tablespoon julienned fresh ginger
2 spring onions (scallions), cut into 3 cm (1^1/$_4$ inch) lengths
500 ml (2 cups) chicken stock*
300 g (10^1/$_2$ oz) daikon, peeled, cut into 5 cm (2 inch) lengths and quartered
3 Chinese cabbage leaves, sliced crossways into 3 cm (1^1/$_4$ inch) lengths
2 tablespoons light soy sauce
2 tablespoons dark soy sauce
^{1}/$_2$ teaspoon sugar
^{1}/$_4$ teaspoon sesame oil

To serve
2 tablespoons chopped coriander (cilantro) leaves

Serves 4–6

In separate bowls, soak the lily buds, mushrooms, fungus and beancurd sticks in hot water for 20–30 minutes, or until softened. Drain, then cut off and discard the mushroom stems.

Heat the oil in a hot wok. Add the garlic, ginger and spring onions and stir-fry for about 30 seconds, or until fragrant. Add the stock, lily buds, mushrooms, fungus, beancurd sticks and daikon and bring to the boil. Reduce the heat and simmer for 5 minutes before adding the Chinese cabbage, soy sauces and sugar. Cover and simmer for 3 minutes. Stir in the sesame oil.

To serve, spoon the braised vegetables and broth into shallow bowls and garnish with coriander leaves.

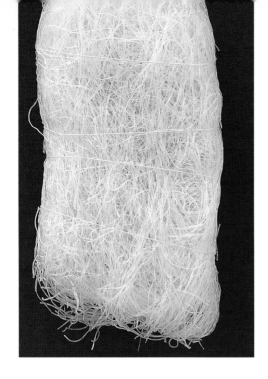

Bean thread vermicelli, more poetically called glass or cellophane noodles, are often sold in a tangled nest. The noodles are usually soaked before use.

Chicken noodle soup

2 litres (8 cups) chicken stock*
2 chicken breast fillets, skinless
1 celery stalk, roughly chopped
5 white peppercorns
1/2 onion, peeled
200 g (7 oz) bean thread vermicelli
11/2 tablespoons fish sauce
1/2 teaspoon sugar
90 g (1 cup) bean sprouts, trimmed
12 g (1/4 bunch) garlic chives, cut into
3 cm (11/4 inch) lengths

To serve
1 handful coriander (cilantro) leaves
2 tablespoons fried shallots*
fish sauce

Serves 6–8

Bring the stock to the boil in a stockpot or large saucepan. Carefully lower the chicken into the pot. Add the celery, peppercorns and onion and return to the boil. Reduce the heat and simmer gently for 5 minutes. Turn off the heat. Cover the stockpot with a tight lid and leave the chicken to cool in the liquid for 20 minutes—it will continue to cook during this time.

Meanwhile, soak the bean thread vermicelli in cold water for 10 minutes, then drain. Cut into 12 cm (5 inch) lengths.

Lift the chicken out of the stock and allow it to cool completely, reserving the stock. Shred the chicken meat and set it aside. Strain the stock and return to the pot. Bring to the boil and season with the fish sauce, sugar and 1/2 teaspoon salt. Divide the noodles among six or eight serving bowls. Top with the shredded chicken and then with the bean sprouts and garlic chives. Pour on the hot stock, then sprinkle with coriander leaves and fried shallots. Serve extra fish sauce, to taste.

The way I stir-fry noodles is to preheat a wok until it is hot enough to impart a smoky, slightly charred flavour to the noodles.

Barbecued pork hokkien noodles

300 g (10^1/$_2$ oz) hokkien (egg) noodles
3 tablespoons vegetable oil
2 garlic cloves, crushed
150 g (5^1/$_2$ oz) char siu (Chinese barbecued pork), sliced
150 g (5^1/$_2$ oz) bok choy (pak choi), cut into quarters lengthways
1^1/$_2$ tablespoons oyster sauce
1^1/$_2$ tablespoons light soy sauce

To serve
1 very small handful bean sprouts, trimmed
1 spring onion (scallion), finely sliced on the diagonal (optional)

Serves 2–4

Run the hokkien noodles under warm water to separate them.

Heat the oil in a hot wok. Add the crushed garlic and stir-fry briefly (20–30 seconds) until fragrant. Add the noodles and stir-fry for about 1 minute, or until the noodles are slightly soft. Add the char siu and bok choy and stir-fry for a further 1–2 minutes.

Add the oyster sauce, soy sauce, 3 tablespoons water and a pinch of salt and white pepper and stir-fry for about 1 minute, or until the noodles have absorbed most of the juice.

To serve, pile the noodles into a bowl, top with bean sprouts and, if you want, sprinkle with spring onion.

Shrimp paste is one of those flavours, like anchovies, that people either love or loathe. I love it. I use Malaysian shrimp paste, which comes in block form, because I find it has a better flavour than the type sold in jars.

Stir-fried water spinach with chilli sambal

2.5 mm (1/8 inch) slice of shrimp paste
in a block
2 garlic cloves, peeled
2 long red chillies, deseeded and chopped
3 red Asian shallots, peeled and
roughly chopped
400 g (14 oz) water spinach
3 tablespoons vegetable oil
1/2 teaspoon sugar

Serves 2–4

Wrap the shrimp paste in foil and heat for 5 minutes, or until fragrant. Use a mortar and pestle to pound the garlic, chillies, shallots and shrimp paste into a paste. Alternatively, chop the ingredients into a paste using a small food processor.

Discard any tough hollow stems from the water spinach, then cut it into 10 cm (4 inch) lengths crossways. Wash and drain the chopped water spinach. Bring a saucepan of lightly salted water to the boil. Add the water spinach and lightly blanch it for 20–30 seconds. Immediately refresh in cold water and drain well.

Heat the oil in a hot wok. Add the chilli–garlic paste and fry for about 1 minute, or until fragrant. Add the water spinach, sugar and a pinch of salt, to taste. Stir-fry for 2 minutes, then serve immediately.

Thai apple eggplants are much firmer than large eggplants, even after cooking, which makes them perfect for use in curries because they keep their shape. If you can't find them, use a regular eggplant and cut it into pieces.

Green fish curry with Thai apple eggplants

400 g (14 oz) white fish fillets
5 Thai apple eggplants (aubergines)
250 ml (1 cup) coconut cream
5 makrut (kaffir) lime leaves, torn
2 long red chillies, sliced on the diagonal
3 tablespoons fish sauce
1 tablespoon shaved palm sugar
8 white peppercorns, crushed
1/2 teaspoon ground coriander
1/4 teaspoon ground cumin
1/4 teaspoon ground turmeric
500 ml (2 cups) coconut milk
8 fresh baby corn
1 handful Thai basil leaves

Curry paste
3 coriander (cilantro) roots
1 teaspoon shrimp paste
4 garlic cloves, peeled
2 red Asian shallots, peeled
1 tablespoon makrut (kaffir) lime zest
3 long green chillies, deseeded and chopped
1 lemon grass stem (white part only), sliced
2 tablespoons sliced fresh galangal

Serves 4

Cut each fish fillet in half lengthways. Trim the eggplants, then cut them in half.

To make the green curry paste, clean the coriander root, then chop. Heat a frying pan over high heat. Wrap the shrimp paste in foil and heat for 5 minutes, or until fragrant. Cool. Put the shrimp paste into a mortar and pestle with the garlic, shallots, coriander roots, lime zest, chillies, lemon grass, galangal and a pinch of salt and pound to a fine paste, adding a little water if necessary. Alternatively, chop the ingredients into a paste using a small food processor.

Scoop the coconut cream into a saucepan and bring to the boil, then simmer for 5–10 minutes, or until the cream separates and a layer of oil forms on the surface.

Add the curry paste to the saucepan and cook for 5–10 minutes, or until fragrant. Add the lime leaves, chillies, fish sauce, sugar, peppercorns, ground coriander, cumin and turmeric and simmer for 2 minutes. Add the coconut milk, eggplants, fish and baby corn and gently simmer for 7–8 minutes, or until the fish is cooked. Stir in the basil leaves, then serve.

The soft, velvety texture of cooked rice noodles is only one of their charms. They also absorb the flavours of the food with which they are cooked.

Stir-fried rice noodles with lap cheong and prawns

2 tablespoons vegetable oil
1/4 onion, sliced
4 king prawns (shrimp), peeled and deveined, tails intact
4–5 slices ready-made fish cakes
1 lap cheong (Chinese sausage), sliced
2 eggs, lightly beaten
250 g (9 oz) fresh rice noodle sheets, cut into 1 cm (1/2 inch) strips
1 spring onion (scallion), cut into 3 cm (11/4 inch) lengths
1 tablespoon light soy sauce
2 tablespoons dark soy sauce
90 g (1 cup) bean sprouts, trimmed

To serve
1 teaspoon roasted sesame seeds*

Serves 1–2

Heat the oil in a hot wok. Add the onion and prawns and stir-fry for about 3 minutes, or until the prawns are nearly cooked. Add the slices of fish cake and sausage and stir-fry for 30 seconds. Pour in the eggs, then add the noodles and spring onion. Cook for 1–2 minutes, or until the noodles soften and the eggs are cooked. Add both the light and dark soy sauces, bean sprouts and a pinch of white pepper, then stir-fry for another 1 minute.

To serve, pile the noodles on a plate or in a bowl and sprinkle with roasted sesame seeds.

Rendang has much less sauce than most other curries and is known as a 'dry' curry. It is traditionally made with beef, but I prefer to make it with chicken.

Rendang chicken curry

250 ml (1 cup) coconut cream
4 tablespoons roasted shredded coconut*
500 ml (2 cups) coconut milk
4 makrut (kaffir) lime leaves, torn
1 teaspoon ground coriander
$1/4$ teaspoon ground turmeric
500 g (1 lb 2 oz) chicken thigh fillet, cut into 5 cm (2 inch) pieces
1 tablespoon shaved palm sugar
2 tablespoons fish sauce

Curry paste
8 dried long red chillies
4 garlic cloves, peeled and roughly chopped
8 red Asian shallots, peeled and roughly chopped
1 lemon grass stem (white part only), sliced
5 cm (2 inch) knob of fresh ginger, chopped
1 tablespoon sliced fresh galangal

To serve
roasted shredded coconut*

Serves 4

To make the curry paste, soak the chillies in hot water for 1–2 minutes, or until softened. Remove the stems and seeds. Use a mortar and pestle to pound all the curry paste ingredients and a pinch of salt into a fine paste, adding a little water if necessary. Alternatively, chop the ingredients into a paste using a small food processor.

Pour the coconut cream into a saucepan and bring to the boil. Boil for about 5 minutes, or until the oil separates from the solids. Add the curry paste and cook for 5–10 minutes, or until fragrant. Add the shredded coconut, coconut milk, lime leaves, coriander and turmeric and simmer for 5 minutes. Add the chicken, sugar, fish sauce and a pinch of salt and cook for 40 minutes, or until the liquid reduces to one-third and the chicken is tender. This curry should be quite dry, but if it becomes too dry, stir in a little extra water. Garnish with extra roasted coconut, then serve.

97

Oxtail imparts a rich, strong flavour to this soup that can't be replicated by using beef bones. Serve the soup with lime wedges to cut through the robust, meaty flavour.

Vietnamese beef and rice noodle soup

1.5 kg (3 lb 5 oz) oxtail, chopped
1.5 kg (3 lb 5 oz) beef brisket
2 knobs of fresh ginger, bruised
2 onions, unpeeled
7 star anise
2 cinnamon sticks
8 cloves
2 cardamom pods
3 tablespoons fish sauce
1 tablespoon sugar
900 g (2 lb) fresh, 1 cm (1/2 inch) wide rice noodles
300 g (10 1/2 oz) beef fillet or silverside, very finely sliced

To serve
205 g (2 1/4 cups) bean sprouts, trimmed
4 spring onions (scallions), finely sliced
2 handfuls mixed herbs, such as coriander (cilantro) and Thai basil leaves
lime wedges

Serves 6–8

Three-quarters fill a stockpot or large saucepan with water and bring to the boil. Add the oxtail and brisket and boil for 3–4 minutes, then drain. Rinse the meat. Pour 5 litres (20 cups) water into a clean stockpot. Add the oxtail and brisket and bring to the boil.

Preheat a chargrill pan or barbecue hotplate over medium–high heat. Cook the ginger and onion until brown all over. Add to the stock along with the star anise, cinnamon sticks, cloves and cardamom pods. Bring the stock to the boil, then reduce the heat to a gentle simmer. Cook for 2 hours, then remove the brisket from the stock. Allow the brisket to cool, then slice thinly and set aside.

Continue to simmer the stock for a further 1 hour, occasionally skimming the fat from the surface. Strain the stock through a sieve and discard the oxtail and spices. Return the stock to the cleaned pot and add the fish sauce, sugar and 1 teaspoon salt. Bring to a gentle simmer.

Pour boiling water over the noodles to soften, then drain.

To serve, divide the noodles among six or eight bowls and top with slices of brisket and the slices of beef fillet or silverside. Pour on the hot stock and garnish with bean sprouts, spring onions and herbs. Serve lime wedges on the side for squeezing over the soup.

This dish has its origins in China, though the Thais adopted it and soon made it their own. It is now one of the most common street foods in Thailand. If you're unable to find noodles that are the right width, buy a block of uncut noodles and cut them into thin strips yourself.

Fried rice noodles with beef and Chinese broccoli

3 tablespoons vegetable oil
250 g (9 oz) fresh, 1 cm (1/2 inch) wide rice noodles
1 tablespoon oyster sauce
1 tablespoon dark soy sauce
1 garlic clove, crushed
60 g (21/4 oz) beef fillet or sirloin, finely sliced
125 ml (1/2 cup) fish stock or water
150 g (1/2 bunch) young Chinese broccoli, cut into 3 cm (11/4 inch) lengths
1 tablespoon cornflour (cornstarch)
1 tablespoon light soy sauce
1 tablespoon dark soy sauce, extra

To serve
1 small handful coriander (cilantro) leaves

Serves 1–2

Heat 2 tablespoons of the oil in a hot wok. Add the noodles and stir-fry for about 1 minute. Add the oyster sauce and dark soy sauce and stir-fry for a further 30 seconds. Remove the noodles from the wok and keep warm.

Heat the remaining tablespoon of oil in a hot wok. Add the garlic and stir-fry briefly (20–30 seconds) until fragrant. Add the beef and stir-fry for about 1 minute before adding the stock and broccoli. Bring the liquid to the boil.

Meanwhile, mix the cornflour with 1 tablespoon water. When the stock in the wok is boiling, add the light soy sauce, extra dark soy sauce and a pinch of salt. Slowly pour in the cornflour mixture, stirring constantly until the sauce thickens.

To serve, put the warm noodles in a shallow bowl. Spoon the beef and broccoli over the noodles and sprinkle with coriander leaves and a pinch of ground white pepper.

101

As a child I used to love visiting the zoo in Saigon (Ho Chi Minh City). The street leading to the zoo was shaded by a row of mature tamarind trees. My brothers and I would pick up the ripe, fallen pods and suck on the sour flesh surrounding the seeds before spitting out the seeds themselves. Perhaps that explains why I love tamarind's sour tang.

Braised duck with tamarind sauce

1 quantity master stock*
1.8 kg (4 lb) whole duck, trimmed and cleaned
vegetable oil, for deep-frying

Sauce
2 tablespoons tamarind paste*
1 tablespoon fish sauce
1 tablespoon shaved palm sugar

To serve
lime halves

Serves 4–6

Pour the master stock into a stockpot or a large saucepan and bring to the boil. Slowly lower the duck in, breast-side down, until fully submerged. Reduce the heat and simmer for 30 minutes. Cover with a lid and turn off the heat. Leave the duck to completely cool in the stock—it will continue to cook during this time. Carefully remove the duck from the liquid and refrigerate the duck overnight. Reserve 250 ml (1 cup) of the master stock to use in the sauce.

To make the sauce, combine all the ingredients and the reserved stock in a small saucepan and bring to the boil. Keep boiling until the sauce is reduced by one-third. Turn off the heat but keep the pan on the stovetop to keep the sauce warm.

Cut the duck in half through the backbone and breastbone. Fill a wok or deep-fat fryer two-thirds full of oil and heat to 170–180°C (325–350°F), or until a cube of bread dropped into the oil browns in 15–20 seconds. Deep-fry the duck one piece at a time for 4–5 minutes, or until the skin is golden brown. Drain on paper towels.

To serve, chop the duck into pieces with a cleaver, arrange on a plate and pour on the sauce. Garnish with lime halves.

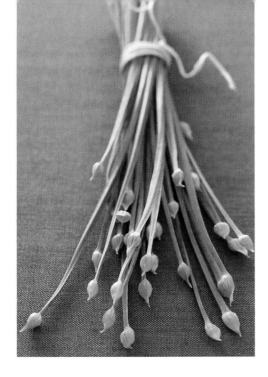

It is easy to make this a vegetarian meal by replacing the chicken stock with vegetable.

Stir-fried tofu, bean sprouts and garlic chives

vegetable oil, for deep-frying
300 g (10^1/$_2$ oz) silken tofu, drained and carefully cut into 3 cm (1^1/$_4$ inch) cubes
2 garlic cloves, crushed
270 g (3 cups) bean sprouts, trimmed
25 g (^{1}/$_2$ bunch) garlic chives, cut into 4 cm (1^1/$_2$ inch) lengths
1 tablespoon light soy sauce
1 tablespoon oyster sauce
2 tablespoons chicken stock*

Serves 2–4

Fill a wok or deep-fat fryer one-third full of oil and heat to 180°C (350°F), or until a cube of bread dropped into the oil browns in 15 seconds. Add the tofu in two batches and deep-fry for 2 minutes, or until golden. Remove and drain on paper towels. Clean out the wok, reserving 2 tablespoons of the oil.

Heat the reserved oil in the wok. Add the garlic and stir-fry briefly (20–30 seconds) until fragrant. Add the bean sprouts, chives, soy sauce, oyster sauce and stock and stir-fry for about 1 minute. Toss in the fried tofu and stir to combine. Serve immediately.

The earthy flavour of this dish comes from dried shiitake mushrooms. When dried, the flavour of the mushrooms intensifies. If you can't find dried, you can use fresh shiitake or even button mushrooms instead.

Stir-fried egg noodles with prawns and vegetables

2 dried shiitake mushrooms
200 g (7 oz) fresh egg noodles
2 tablespoons vegetable oil
8 prawns (shrimp), peeled and deveined, tails intact
1 garlic clove, crushed
1 teaspoon finely grated fresh ginger
3 Chinese cabbage leaves, finely sliced
1/2 carrot, julienned
2 tablespoons chicken stock*
1 tablespoon light soy sauce
1 1/2 tablespoons oyster sauce
1/2 teaspoon sesame oil
12 g (1/4 bunch) garlic chives, cut into 3 cm (1 1/4 inch) lengths

To serve
coriander (cilantro) leaves
lime wedges

Serves 2–4

Soak the mushrooms in hot water for 20 minutes, then drain. Discard the stems and finely slice the caps.

Cook the noodles in boiling water for 1 minute. Drain, then refresh under cold running water. Drain again. Heat the oil in a hot wok. Add the prawns and stir-fry for about 3 minutes, or until nearly cooked. Add the garlic and ginger and stir-fry until fragrant. Toss in the cabbage, mushrooms and carrot and stir-fry until the cabbage starts to wilt. Add the noodles and stir-fry for 1 minute. Add the stock, soy sauce, oyster sauce, sesame oil and garlic chives and stir-fry for a further 1 minute.

To serve, pile the noodles on a plate and garnish with coriander leaves and serve with lime wedges.

The trick to achieving the crispiest possible skin is to cook the chicken twice. First poach the chicken in stock, then leave it to cool so the flesh is moist and flavoursome. Next briefly deep-fry it to make the skin crunchy.

Crispy skinned chicken with chilli and basil sauce

1 quantity master stock*
1.5 kg (3 lb 5 oz) whole chicken
vegetable oil, for deep-frying

Sauce
1 garlic clove, peeled
1 long red chilli, deseeded and chopped
2 tablespoons light soy sauce
pinch of sugar
1 tablespoon mirin
2 tablespoons black vinegar
2 tablespoons grapeseed oil
6–8 Thai basil leaves, shredded
2 tablespoons spring onions (scallions), finely sliced

Serves 2–4

Pour the master stock into a stockpot or large saucepan and bring to the boil. Slowly lower in the chicken, breast-side down, until fully submerged. Reduce the heat and simmer for 15 minutes. Cover with a lid and turn off the heat. Leave the chicken in the stock for 3 hours— it will continue to cook during this time. Carefully remove the chicken from the stock. Allow to cool completely, then refrigerate overnight.

To make the sauce, use a mortar and pestle to pound the garlic and chopped chilli together. Work in the rest of the ingredients, pounding until the sugar dissolves. Alternatively, finely chop the garlic and chilli, then put in a small bowl and mix in the rest of the ingredients.

Cut the chicken in half through the backbone and breastbone. Fill a wok or deep-fat fryer two-thirds full of oil and heat to 170°C (325°F), or until a cube of bread dropped into the oil browns in 20 seconds. Carefully lower one piece of chicken at a time into the oil and deep-fry, turning occasionally, for 8–10 minutes, or until the skin is golden brown and crispy. Remove from the wok and drain on paper towels.

To serve, chop the chicken into smaller pieces with a cleaver, arrange on a plate, then drizzle the sauce over the top.

Scallops are quite hard to get in many Asian countries and, consequently, they are very expensive. Now that I enjoy the luxury of buying them whenever I like, I've added them to this otherwise classic Chinese stir-fry.

Stir-fried scallops with chilli and black beans

300 g (10½ oz) scallops, roe removed
4 tablespoons vegetable oil
1 tablespoon fermented black beans
2 garlic cloves, crushed
¼ onion, sliced
3 spring onions (scallions), cut into
6 cm (2½ inch) lengths
2 long red chillies, deseeded and sliced
10 baby corn, sliced in half lengthways
3 tablespoons chicken stock*
2 tablespoons light soy sauce
2 tablespoons Shaoxing rice wine
1 teaspoon caster (superfine) sugar

To serve
2 tablespoons coriander (cilantro) leaves
2 tablespoons spring onions (scallions),
sliced on the diagonal

Serves 2–4

Slice the small, hard white muscle off the side of each scallop and pull off any membrane. Rinse the scallops, then pat dry.

Heat the oil in a hot wok. Add the scallops and stir-fry for 1–2 minutes, or until nearly cooked. Remove the scallops from the wok using a slotted spoon and set aside.

Add the black beans, garlic, onion, spring onions and chillies and stir-fry for about 1 minute. Return the scallops to the wok along with the baby corn. Stir-fry for 1 minute. Add the stock, soy sauce, wine and sugar and simmer for a further 2 minutes.

To serve, scoop the scallops on to a plate and garnish with coriander leaves and spring onions.

Most young coconuts are imported from Vietnam and Thailand. The juice from these smooth coconuts has a beautifully subtle taste. If you're not lucky enough to find fresh coconuts, the juice is available in tins. Don't buy a tin of coconut milk, which is made from the crushed and squeezed flesh of a coconut.

Braised pork with young coconut and water spinach

1 kg (2 lb 4 oz) leg pork
4 tablespoons vegetable oil
3 garlic cloves, crushed
3 red Asian shallots, sliced
100 ml (3^1/$_2$ fl oz) fish sauce
2 tablespoons caramel syrup*
750 ml (3 cups) young coconut juice
250 ml (1 cup) chicken stock*
6 hard-boiled eggs, peeled
60 g (1/2 bunch) water spinach

To serve
3 spring onions (scallions), julienned on the diagonal

Serves 4–6

Slice the pork into thick slices, about 5 cm (2 inches) long, 2 cm (^{3}/$_4$ inch) thick and 3 cm (1^1/$_4$ inches) wide.

Heat 1 tablespoon of the oil in a hot wok, then cook the pork in batches for 2–3 minutes, or until browned, adding more oil as necessary. Remove from the wok.

Heat 1 tablespoon of the oil in a saucepan and fry the garlic and shallots until fragrant. Add the pork, fish sauce, caramel syrup and a pinch of salt and white pepper. Stir well over medium heat for 2 minutes. Add the coconut juice and stock and bring to the boil. Reduce the heat and simmer gently, covered, for 1^1/$_2$ hours, or until the pork is tender. Add the eggs and simmer for 15 minutes. Add the water spinach and simmer for a further 3 minutes.

To serve, carefully remove the eggs from the sauce and cut them in half. Place the water spinach and eggs in a shallow bowl. Top with the pork and sauce, then sprinkle with spring onions.

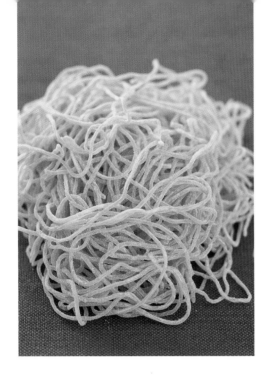

Noodles are often used to soak up the flavour of other ingredients, but they can also be fried to provide crunch, as they are here.

Crispy noodles with chicken and vegetables

vegetable oil, for deep-frying
200 g (7 oz) fresh thin egg noodles
1 garlic clove, crushed
100 g (3¹/₂ oz) skinless chicken breast fillet, sliced
150 g (1 bunch) asparagus, sliced on the diagonal
2 bok choy (pak choi), cut into quarters lengthways
150 g (5¹/₂ oz) snow peas (mangetout), trimmed
4 large oyster mushrooms, roughly torn
125 ml (¹/₂ cup) chicken stock*
3 tablespoons Shaoxing rice wine
1 tablespoon light soy sauce
1 tablespoon dark soy sauce
2 teaspoons sugar
¹/₂ teaspoon sesame oil
1 tablespoon cornflour (cornstarch)

To serve
coriander (cilantro) leaves

Serves 2–4

Fill a wok or deep-fat fryer one-third full of oil and heat to 180°C (350°F), or until a cube of bread dropped into the oil browns in 15 seconds. Carefully add the noodles and fry for 20–30 seconds, or until puffed and golden. Drain on paper towels and keep warm. Clean out the wok, reserving 1 tablespoon of the oil.

Heat the reserved oil in a hot wok. Add the garlic and stir-fry briefly (20–30 seconds) until fragrant. Add the chicken and stir-fry for 1–2 minutes, or until the chicken is nearly cooked through. Add all the vegetables and stir-fry for about 3 minutes, or until the vegetables just start to wilt but are still crisp. Transfer to a warm dish.

Clean out the wok and pour in the stock, wine, light soy sauce, dark soy sauce, sugar, sesame oil and 1 teaspoon salt. Bring to the boil.

Meanwhile, combine the cornflour with 1 tablespoon water. Add the chicken and vegetables to the wok, then pour in the cornflour mixture, stirring constantly until the sauce thickens.

To serve, put the crispy noodles in a bowl and top with the chicken and vegetables. Garnish with coriander leaves and sprinkle with a pinch of ground white pepper.

This may be a simpler version of Pad Thai than you are used to, but it's the classic recipe for what is arguably Thailand's most famous noodle export.

Pad Thai

150 g (5$^{1}/_{2}$ oz) thin dried rice noodles
1 tablespoon dried shrimp
vegetable oil, for deep-frying
50 g (1$^{3}/_{4}$ oz) firm tofu, cut into thin,
2 cm ($^{3}/_{4}$ inch) long strips
$^{1}/_{4}$ onion, finely sliced
2 eggs, lightly beaten
90 g (1 cup) bean sprouts, trimmed
25 g ($^{1}/_{2}$ bunch) garlic chives, cut into
2 cm ($^{3}/_{4}$ inch) lengths

Sauce
1$^{1}/_{2}$ tablespoons fish sauce
1 tablespoon shaved palm sugar
1 tablespoon tamarind water*
1 tablespoon oyster sauce

To serve
1 tablespoon ground roasted peanuts*
lime wedges

Serves 1–2

Soak the noodles in cold water for 30 minutes, or until softened. Drain. Meanwhile, soak the dried shrimp in hot water for 10–15 minutes, or until softened. Drain, then chop.

Fill a wok or deep-fat fryer one-third full of oil and heat to 180°C (350°F), or until a cube of bread dropped into the oil browns in 15 seconds. Deep-fry the tofu for 1 minute, or until lightly golden. Drain on paper towels. Clean out the wok, reserving 1 tablespoon of the oil.

To make the sauce, put the fish sauce, palm sugar, tamarind water and oyster sauce in a small saucepan and simmer gently until the sugar dissolves.

Heat the reserved oil in a hot wok. Add the onion and stir-fry for about 1 minute, or until fragrant. Stir in the beaten eggs, then add the tofu, dried shrimp and noodles and stir-fry for about 1 minute. Add the sauce and simmer for 30 seconds. Add the bean sprouts and garlic chives and stir-fry for a further 30 seconds.

To serve, pile the noodles on a plate and sprinkle with ground roasted peanuts. Serve with lime wedges.

I discovered sambals while travelling in Malaysia. Essentially a chilli sauce, some sambals are used as a marinade or for stir-frying, while others are served as an accompanying relish.

Sambal squid

300 g (10¹/₂ oz) squid tubes
3 tablespoons vegetable oil
10 snow peas (mangetout), trimmed
8 baby corn, halved
2 tablespoons tamarind water*
1¹/₂ tablespoons shaved palm sugar
2 tablespoons fish sauce

Sambal paste
1 teaspoon shrimp paste
4 dried red chillies
2 garlic cloves, peeled
3 red Asian shallots, peeled
2 long red chillies, deseeded and chopped

To serve
2 tablespoons coriander (cilantro) leaves

Serves 2–4

Open up the squid tubes and scrub off any soft jelly-like substance, then score the inside of the flesh with a fine crisscross pattern, making sure you do not cut all the way through. Cut the squid into 2 x 5 cm (³/₄ x 2 inch) pieces.

To make the sambal paste, heat a frying pan over high heat. Wrap the shrimp paste in foil and heat for 5 minutes, or until fragrant. Cool. Soak the dried chillies in hot water for 1–2 minutes, then drain. Remove the stems and seeds, then roughly chop. Use a mortar and pestle to pound the shrimp paste, dried chillies, garlic, shallots and fresh chillies into a paste. Alternatively, chop the ingredients into a paste using a small food processor.

Heat the oil in a hot wok and stir-fry the squid in two batches for 2 minutes. Remove the squid and set aside. In the same wok, fry the paste for 1–2 minutes, or until fragrant. Return the squid to the wok along with the snow peas, corn, tamarind water, palm sugar and fish sauce and stir-fry for 2 minutes.

To serve, scoop the squid sambal into a serving bowl and sprinkle with some coriander leaves.

As far as I know no-one else adds mustard greens to a curry. I love the combination because mustard greens have a slightly sour taste that sets off the sweetness of the coconut milk.

Lamb curry

40 g (¹/4 cup) raw cashew nuts
3 tablespoons vegetable oil
500 g (1 lb 2 oz) leg lamb, cut into
3 cm (1¹/4 inch) cubes
1 small tomato, diced
500 ml (2 cups) coconut milk
250 ml (1 cup) coconut cream
1 tablespoon shaved palm sugar
1 tablespoon fish sauce

Spice mix
2 cardamom pods
1 cinnamon stick
2 teaspoons ground coriander
¹/2 teaspoon ground cumin
¹/4 teaspoon freshly grated nutmeg
¹/2 teaspoon ground turmeric
¹/4 teaspoon ground fennel
8 white peppercorns, crushed

Curry paste
5 dried long red chillies
6 red Asian shallots, peeled and
roughly chopped
2 garlic cloves, peeled and roughly
chopped
1 tablespoon sliced lemon grass
(white part only)
1 tablespoon sliced fresh galangal

To serve
40 g (¹/4 cup) finely sliced pickled
mustard greens
1 long red chilli, deseeded and sliced

Serves 6

Blanch the cashew nuts in boiling water for 4–5 minutes, or until soft, then drain. Use a mortar and pestle to crush them.

To make the spice mix, heat a small frying pan over high heat. Add the cardamom pods and cinnamon stick and dry-fry for about 2 minutes, or until fragrant. Cool slightly, then use a mortar and pestle to finely grind them. Mix in the rest of the ingredients.

To make the curry paste, soak the chillies in hot water for 1–2 minutes, or until softened. Remove the stems and seeds. Use a mortar and pestle to pound all the paste ingredients into a purée, adding a little water if necessary. Alternatively, chop the ingredients into a paste using a small food processor.

Heat the oil in a saucepan. Add the curry paste and fry for 2 minutes, or until fragrant. Add the spice mix and cook, stirring, for 2–3 minutes. Add the lamb and tomato and stir-fry until the meat is well coated. Stir in the coconut milk, coconut cream and ground cashew nuts. Bring to the boil, then reduce the heat to low and simmer for 1 hour. Add the sugar, fish sauce and a pinch of salt and simmer for an extra 5 minutes, or until the meat is tender and the curry is thick.

To serve, spoon the lamb curry into a bowl and garnish with mustard greens and sliced red chilli.

Chinese broccoli with yellow bean sauce

300 g (1 bunch) Chinese broccoli
2 tablespoons vegetable oil
1 garlic clove, crushed
1 tablespoon yellow bean sauce
1 tablespoon finely sliced fresh ginger
2 teaspoons sugar

Serves 2–4

Wash and drain the Chinese broccoli, then trim the stems and cut each stem in half crossways.

Heat the oil in a saucepan. Add the garlic and fry briefly (20–30 seconds) until fragrant. Add the yellow bean sauce, ginger and sugar and simmer for 1 minute. Remove from the heat and set aside.

Bring a saucepan of water to the boil, add the broccoli and simmer for 1–2 minutes, or until tender. Drain and cut into 4–5 cm (1$\frac{1}{2}$–2 inch) lengths. Serve the broccoli on a plate and pour the sauce over the top.

Bok choy with garlic and oyster sauce

300 g (10$\frac{1}{2}$ oz) bok choy (pak choi), washed, cut into quarters lengthways
2 garlic cloves, finely crushed
2 tablespoons vegetable oil
2 tablespoons oyster sauce

Serves 2–4

Bring a saucepan of salted water to the boil. Add the bok choy and simmer for 1 minute, or until just cooked. Remove from the water and drain well. Arrange on a serving plate.

Heat the oil in a small frying pan. Add the garlic and fry briefly (20–30 seconds) until light brown. Remove from the heat and stir in the oyster sauce. Drizzle over the bok choy and serve immediately.

In Vietnam, soups like this are eaten throughout the day, no matter what the season. This soup has a particularly restorative feel.

Crabmeat and rice vermicelli soup

400 g (14 oz) dried rice vermicelli
250 g (9 oz) cooked crabmeat
3 eggs, lightly beaten
3 tablespoons vegetable oil
1 small leek, finely sliced
1/2 teaspoon shrimp paste (optional)
4 tomatoes, cut into wedges
1.5–2 litres (6–8 cups) chicken stock*
12 tofu puffs, each cut in half
3 tablespoons fish sauce
2 tablespoons tamarind water*

Paste
60 g (1/2 cup) dried shrimp
2 garlic cloves, peeled
2 long red chillies, deseeded and chopped

To serve
4 spring onions (scallions), finely sliced
1/4 small white cabbage, finely shredded
180 g (2 cups) bean sprouts, trimmed
1 handful coriander (cilantro) leaves
1 handful mint leaves
lime wedges

Serves 6–8

Put the vermicelli in a bowl and cover with boiling water. Leave to soften for 5–7 minutes, then drain. Refresh under cold water, then drain again. Combine the crabmeat and eggs and mix well.

To make the paste, soak the dried shrimp in hot water for 10–15 minutes, or until softened. Drain. Use a mortar and pestle to pound the garlic, chillies and dried shrimp into a paste. Alternatively, chop the ingredients into a paste using a small food processor.

Heat the oil in a stockpot or large saucepan. Add the paste and fry for 1–2 minutes, or until fragrant. Add the leek and fry for 30 seconds. Add the shrimp paste (if you are using it) and tomato and stir-fry until the shrimp paste separates. Pour in the stock and bring to the boil.

Reduce the stock to a gentle simmer. Spoon the crabmeat mixture into the stock, a spoonful at a time—the egg should bind the crabmeat into loose balls. Toss in the tofu puffs and season with the fish sauce, tamarind water and 1 teaspoon salt.

To serve, divide the vermicelli among six or eight deep serving bowls. Pour on the hot stock. Garnish with the spring onions, cabbage, bean sprouts, coriander and mint. Serve the lime wedges on the side for squeezing over the soup.

The Thais have long recognized how useful the natural acidity of tamarind is as a souring agent. I also use it to cut through the fatty flavour of meat.

Braised beef brisket with chilli and tamarind sauce

400 g (14 oz) beef brisket

Braising stock
3 tablespoons dark soy sauce
3 tablespoons light soy sauce
8 garlic cloves, peeled and bruised
5 cm (2 inch) knob of fresh ginger, bruised
2 lemon grass stems, bruised
3 tablespoons sugar
4 makrut (kaffir) lime leaves, torn
1 teaspoon white pepper

Sauce
1 bird's eye chilli, finely sliced
4 tablespoons tamarind water*
1 tablespoon fish sauce
2 tablespoons sugar

To serve
3 tablespoons fried shallots*
2 handfuls coriander (cilantro) leaves
6 spring onions (scallions), julienned
lime wedges

Serves 2–4

Put the beef in a saucepan and pour in enough cold water to submerge it. Bring to the boil. Drain, then rinse the beef under cold running water.

Put the beef in a stockpot or large saucepan. Add all the ingredients for the braising stock plus 1.5 litres (6 cups) water. Bring to the boil, then reduce the heat to a simmer and cook, uncovered, for 2 hours, or until the meat is tender and almost 'melting'. Remove the beef from the stock (reserving the braising stock) and leave to rest for 10 minutes. Slice thinly. Strain the braising stock into a bowl—you need 170 ml (2/3 cup) to use in the sauce.

To make the sauce, combine all the ingredients and the reserved braising stock in a saucepan and bring to the boil. The sauce should taste hot, sour, salty and a little sweet. Add extra tamarind water, fish sauce or sugar, to taste.

To serve, arrange the beef slices on a plate and pour the sauce over the top. Sprinkle with fried shallots, coriander and spring onions and serve with lime wedges.

This is a great dish for the barbecue. You can prepare it in advance and cook it at the last minute.

Chargrilled chicken with lime and chilli sauce

2 x 350–400 g (12–14 oz) small chickens or 4 chicken leg quarters

Marinade
4 garlic cloves, peeled
2 tablespoons cleaned and chopped coriander (cilantro) roots
1 lemon grass stem (white part only), chopped
1 teaspoon finely grated fresh ginger
3 tablespoons fish sauce
2 tablespoons coconut milk
2 tablespoons vegetable oil

Sauce
1 long red chilli, deseeded and finely sliced
2 garlic cloves, sliced
1 tablespoon shaved palm sugar
1–2 tablespoons fish sauce
3 tablespoons lime juice
3 makrut (kaffir) lime leaves, central vein removed, leaves very finely sliced

To serve
2 tablespoons chopped roasted peanuts*

Serves 2–4

If you are using whole chickens, butterfly them by cutting along the backbone. Press down hard on the breastbone to flatten the chicken.

To make the marinade, use a mortar and pestle to pound the garlic, coriander, lemon grass and ginger into a paste. Add the fish sauce, coconut milk and oil and stir until well combined. Alternatively, chop the ingredients into a paste using a small food processor. Scoop into a non-metallic bowl with the chicken. Rub the marinade all over the chicken, then leave to marinate in the refrigerator for 3–4 hours.

Preheat a chargrill pan or barbecue hotplate over medium–low heat. Remove the chicken from the marinade, reserving the marinade. Cook the chicken for 15–20 minutes, or until cooked through. Turn the chicken regularly and baste with the reserved marinade.

To make the sauce, combine all the sauce ingredients and stir until the sugar dissolves.

To serve, chop the chicken with a cleaver and serve the sauce and peanuts in small bowls on the side.

129

Duck is a fatty meat so it's best served with something sour, like pineapple, to cut through its richness.

Duck and pineapple curry

625 ml (2¹/₂ cups) coconut milk
1 Chinese roasted duck, boned and cut
into 2 cm (³/₄ inch) chunks
125 ml (¹/₂ cup) chicken stock*
1 tablespoon shaved palm sugar
2 tablespoons fish sauce
30 g (1 oz) snake beans, cut into 4 cm
(1¹/₂ inch) lengths
5 makrut (kaffir) lime leaves, torn
8 cherry tomatoes, halved
70 g (¹/₃ cup) pineapple pieces
1 handful Thai basil leaves

Curry paste
6 dried long red chillies
1 teaspoon shrimp paste
3 garlic cloves, peeled
4 red Asian shallots, peeled
1 lemon grass stem (white part only), sliced
1 tablespoon sliced fresh galangal
1¹/₂ teaspoons ground coriander
1 teaspoon ground cumin
¹/₂ teaspoon paprika
¹/₂ teaspoon ground cloves

Serves 4–6

To make the curry paste, soak the chillies in hot water for 1–2 minutes, or until softened. Remove the stems and seeds and roughly chop. Heat a frying pan over high heat. Wrap the shrimp paste in foil and heat for 5 minutes, or until fragrant. Cool. Use a mortar and pestle to pound the shrimp paste and the rest of the ingredients into a fine paste, adding a little water if necessary. Alternatively, chop the ingredients into a paste using a small food processor.

Put the coconut milk and curry paste in a saucepan and bring to the boil. Reduce the heat and simmer for 5 minutes. Add the duck, stock, sugar, fish sauce, snake beans, lime leaves and a pinch of salt and simmer for 5 minutes. Add the tomatoes and pineapple and cook for another 3 minutes. Just before serving, stir in the basil leaves.

Stir-fried tofu, snow peas and baby corn

vegetable oil, for deep-frying
300 g (10¹/₂ oz) silken tofu, drained and
cut into 3 cm (1¹/₄ inch) cubes
2 garlic cloves, crushed
100 g (3¹/₂ oz) snow peas (mangetout),
trimmed
10 baby corn, halved lengthways
2 tablespoons oyster sauce
1 tablespoon Shaoxing rice wine
3 tablespoons chicken stock*

Serves 2–4

Fill a wok or deep-fat fryer one-third full of oil and heat to 180°C (350°F), or until a cube of bread dropped into the oil browns in 15 seconds. Add the tofu in three batches and deep-fry for 2 minutes, or until golden. Drain on paper towels and set aside. Clean out the wok, reserving 2 tablespoons of the oil.

Heat the reserved oil in a hot wok. Add the garlic and stir-fry briefly (20–30 seconds) until fragrant. Add the snow peas and baby corn and stir-fry for 1 minute. Pour in the oyster sauce, wine and stock and stir-fry for another 1 minute. Toss in the deep-fried tofu and gently stir-fry for 30 seconds. Serve immediately.

Stir-fried broccolini with chilli paste

400 g (2 bunches) broccolini, cut into
8 cm (3 inch) lengths
2 tablespoons vegetable oil
1 garlic clove, crushed
2 tablespoons chicken stock*
3 tablespoons chilli jam*

Serves 2–4

Lightly blanch the broccolini in boiling water for 30 seconds. Drain, refresh in cold water immediately and drain again.

Heat the oil in a hot wok. Add the garlic and stir-fry briefly (20–30 seconds) until fragrant. Add the broccolini, chicken stock and chilli jam and stir-fry for 1 minute, or until the broccolini is well coated.

This dish improves with age. Cook it a day in advance, leave it to cool in the refrigerator, then reheat as you need it. The flavours will intensify overnight.

Braised five-spice chicken with Chinese broccoli

3 tablespoons vegetable oil
400 g (14 oz) chicken thigh fillet, sliced crossways into thin 4 cm (1¹/₂ inch) lengths
2 garlic cloves, crushed
3 red Asian shallots, sliced
2 tablespoons fish sauce
2 tablespoons light soy sauce
3 tablespoons caramel syrup*
generous pinch of five-spice powder
40 g (1¹/₂ oz) Chinese broccoli, chopped into 3 cm (1¹/₄ inch) pieces

To serve
2 tablespoons coriander (cilantro) leaves
5 red chillies, deseeded and finely sliced

Serves 2–4

Heat 2 tablespoons of the oil in a hot wok. Add the chicken pieces in small batches and cook until browned. Drain and set aside.

Heat the remaining tablespoon of oil in a saucepan. Add the garlic and shallots and fry for about 2–3 minutes, or until fragrant. Add the fish sauce, soy sauce, caramel syrup, five-spice powder, 4 tablespoons water and a pinch of salt and white pepper. Stir well, then add the chicken pieces. Bring to the boil, then reduce the heat and simmer gently for 15 minutes, or until the chicken is tender. Add the broccoli and simmer for another 3 minutes.

To serve, put the broccoli on a plate, sit the chicken pieces on top and spoon on the sauce. Garnish with the coriander leaves and sliced chilli.

I couldn't possibly write a cookbook without including my signature dish, Salt and pepper squid. The secret ingredient is a small pinch of five-spice powder.

Salt and pepper squid

400 g (14 oz) squid tubes
vegetable oil, for deep-frying
4 tablespoons cornflour (cornstarch) or potato starch

Salt and pepper mixture
1 tablespoon salt
1 tablespoon mixed ground black and white pepper
2 teaspoons caster (superfine) sugar
small pinch of five-spice powder

To serve
180 g (2 cups) finely shredded iceberg lettuce
lime halves
2 spring onions (scallions), julienned
1 handful coriander (cilantro) leaves
1 long red chilli, deseeded and julienned

Serves 2

Open up the squid tubes and scrub off any soft jelly-like substance, then score the inside of the flesh with a fine crisscross pattern, making sure you do not cut all the way through. Cut the squid into 2 x 5 cm (3/4 x 2 inch) pieces.

Combine all the ingredients for the salt and pepper mixture in a bowl.

Fill a wok or deep-fat fryer one-half full of oil and heat to 140°C (275°F), or until a cube of bread dropped into the oil browns in about 45 seconds. Coat the squid with cornflour and shake off any excess flour. Deep-fry the squid in small batches for 3–4 minutes, or until crisp. Drain on paper towels. Sprinkle with the salt and pepper mix, making sure the squid is well coated. Store any excess salt and pepper mixture in an airtight container.

To serve, put the shredded lettuce on a plate, top with the salt and pepper squid and put the lime halves on the side. Garnish with spring onions, coriander and chilli.

Stir-fried beef with chilli, asparagus and oyster mushrooms

4 tablespoons vegetable oil
350 g (12 oz) beef fillet, trimmed and finely sliced
8 asparagus spears, trimmed and sliced into 5 cm (2 inch) pieces on the diagonal
8 large fresh oyster mushrooms
1 tablespoon light soy sauce
1 tablespoon oyster sauce
1 teaspoon sugar
3 tablespoons chicken stock*

Paste
3 garlic cloves, peeled
3 tablespoons cleaned and chopped coriander (cilantro) roots
2 long red chillies, deseeded and chopped

Serves 2–4

To make the paste, use a mortar and pestle to pound the garlic, coriander roots, chillies and a pinch of salt together. Alternatively, chop the ingredients into a paste using a small food processor.

Heat the oil in a hot wok, add the beef and the paste and stir-fry for 1–2 minutes. Add the rest of the ingredients and cook for 2 minutes, or until the asparagus is tender.

To serve, pile the beef, asparagus and mushrooms in a bowl and pour the sauce over the top.

Stir-fried beef with chillies and lemon grass

3 tablespoons vegetable oil
350 g (12 oz) beef fillet, trimmed and finely sliced
1 1/2 tablespoons fish sauce
1 teaspoon sugar
4 tablespoons chicken stock*

Paste
3 garlic cloves, peeled
3 red Asian shallots, peeled
2 long red chillies, deseeded and sliced
2 lemon grass stems (white part only), sliced

Serves 2–4

To make the paste, use a mortar and pestle to pound the garlic, shallots, chillies and lemon grass together. Alternatively, chop the ingredients into a paste using a small food processor.

Heat the oil in a hot wok and fry the paste until fragrant. Add the beef and stir-fry for 2–3 minutes. Add the fish sauce, sugar and stock and cook for 2 minutes, or until the beef is cooked.

To serve, pile the beef on a plate and pour the sauce over the top.

Chillies are an everyday part of life in Asia, so people develop a tolerance to their heat over many years. If you're a newcomer to chillies, begin by removing the hottest part, the seeds and membrane. As you become accustomed to their heat you may prefer to leave them in.

Red prawn and pumpkin curry

Curry paste
1 tablespoon shrimp paste
4 garlic cloves
4 red Asian shallots
7 dried long red chillies, deseeded and soaked
1 lemon grass stem (white part only), sliced
2 tablespoons sliced fresh galangal
1 tablespoon chopped coriander (cilantro) root

250 ml (1 cup) coconut cream
2 tablespoons vegetable oil
500 ml (2 cups) coconut milk
300 g (10 1/2 oz) butternut pumpkin (squash), cut into 3 cm (1 1/4 inch) cubes
1 tablespoon shaved palm sugar
2 tablespoons fish sauce
12 king prawns (shrimp), peeled and deveined, tails intact

To serve
3 makrut (kaffir) lime leaves, very finely shredded

Serves 4

To make the curry paste, heat a frying pan over high heat. Wrap the shrimp paste in foil and heat for 5 minutes, or until fragrant. Cool. Put the shrimp paste into a blender with the remaining paste ingredients and process to a purée, adding a little water if necessary.

Put the coconut cream and oil in a saucepan and bring to the boil, stirring constantly, because the coconut cream can burn easily. When the oil has separated from the solids, add the paste and cook until fragrant—this should take 5–10 minutes. Add the coconut milk and pumpkin and cook over a low heat until the pumpkin is tender. Add the sugar, fish sauce, prawns and a pinch of salt and cook for a further 5 minutes.

To serve, spoon the prawn and pumpkin curry into a bowl and scatter with the shredded lime leaves.

141

Swordfish is not a traditional accompaniment to Vietnamese salad but I think the freshness of the salad and the meatiness of the fish make a perfect pairing.

Chargrilled swordfish with chilli jam and Vietnamese salad

300 g (10¹/₂ oz) swordfish steaks, 2 cm (³/₄ inch) thick

Salad
75 g (1 cup) finely shredded white cabbage
1 large carrot, finely julienned
3 red Asian shallots, finely sliced
1 small handful Vietnamese mint leaves
1 small handful coriander (cilantro) leaves
1 quantity nuoc cham (Vietnamese dipping sauce)*

To serve
2 tablespoons chopped roasted peanuts*
1 tablespoon fried shallots*
1–2 tablespoons chilli jam*
a few coriander (cilantro) sprigs
lime wedges

Serves 2–4

Cut the swordfish steaks into strips 12 cm (5 inches) long and 6 cm (2¹/₂ inches) wide. Season the pieces with salt and white pepper. Preheat a chargrill pan or barbecue hotplate over high heat. Cook the swordfish for 2 minutes on each side. Remove from the pan and rest for 2 minutes.

Combine the salad ingredients and moisten with nuoc cham sauce—you may not need to use all the sauce.

To serve, arrange the salad on a plate and sprinkle with the peanuts and fried shallots. Place the fish on top of the salad and top with chilli jam and coriander sprigs. Serve with lime wedges.

You need time to prepare a curry. Time to grind the spices, time to 'crack' the coconut cream and time to allow the flavours to infuse. I tend to make curries on the weekends when I can enjoy the process. If you make extra, it will keep well in the fridge for a couple of days.

Beef and potato curry

2 small potatoes, peeled and quartered
250 ml (1 cup) coconut cream
8 white peppercorns, finely crushed
1 tablespoon ground coriander
2 teaspoons ground cumin
1/2 teaspoon ground fennel
500 ml (2 cups) coconut milk
500 g (1 lb 2 oz) beef blade, trimmed and cut into 3 cm (1 1/4 inch) pieces
1 tablespoon shaved palm sugar
2–3 tablespoons fish sauce

Curry paste
8 dried long red chillies
4 red Asian shallots, roughly chopped
3 garlic cloves, roughly chopped
1 lemon grass stem (white part only), sliced
2 tablespoons sliced fresh galangal

To serve
1 handful fried shallots*

Serves 4

To make the curry paste, soak the chillies in hot water for 1–2 minutes, or until softened. Remove the stems and seeds, then roughly chop. Use a mortar and pestle to pound all the paste ingredients and a pinch of salt into a fine paste. Alternatively, chop the ingredients into a paste using a small food processor.

Cook the potatoes in boiling, salted water for 12–15 minutes, or until cooked but still firm. Drain and set aside.

Scoop the coconut cream into a saucepan and bring to the boil, then simmer for 5–10 minutes, or until the cream 'cracks'—when it separates and a layer of oil forms on the surface. Add the paste and cook for 5–10 minutes, or until fragrant. Stir in the peppercorns, ground coriander, cumin and fennel and mix well. Add the coconut milk, beef, sugar and fish sauce and simmer for 1 1/2–2 hours, or until the beef is tender. Add the potatoes and cook for an extra 5–10 minutes. The sauce should be quite thick, but if it is too thick, stir in a little extra coconut milk and heat through.

To serve, spoon the curry into a bowl and sprinkle with fried shallots.

The saltiness of black beans needs to be counterbalanced by something sweet, such as the slipper lobster meat used here.

Fried slipper lobsters with chilli and black bean sauce

6 slipper lobsters (e.g. Moreton Bay
or Balmain bugs) or scampi,
thawed if frozen
80 g (1/2 cup) potato starch or 60 g
(1/2 cup) cornflour (cornstarch)
150 g (51/2 oz) bok choy (pak choi), washed
and quartered lengthways
vegetable oil, for deep-frying

Sauce
2 tablespoons vegetable oil
11/2 tablespoons salted black beans
2 garlic cloves, crushed
1 long red chilli, sliced
1 spring onion (scallion), sliced
2 tablespoons Shaoxing rice wine
2 tablespoons oyster sauce
1 teaspoon caster (superfine) sugar
4 tablespoons chicken stock*

To serve
1 handful julienned spring onions
(scallions)
1 handful coriander (cilantro) sprigs

Serves 2–4

Holding each slipper lobster, cut into the membrane where the head and body join, to loosen the head, then firmly twist or cut off the tail. Discard the head. Cut down both sides of the underside shell, then peel back the soft shell to reveal the flesh. Gently pull the flesh out in one piece. Discard the shell. Wash and drain well. Dust the lobsters with potato starch, shaking off any excess.

To make the sauce, heat the oil in a hot wok. Add the black beans, garlic, chilli and spring onion and fry for about 1 minute, or until fragrant. Add the wine, oyster sauce, sugar and stock and bring to the boil. Boil until the sauce reduces by one-third. Remove the sauce from the heat and keep warm.

Bring a wok or large saucepan of water to the boil. Put the bok choy in a steamer. Sit the steamer over the wok of boiling water, making sure the base of the steamer does not touch the water. Put the lid on the steamer and steam for 3–4 minutes, or until tender.

Fill a wok or deep-fat fryer one-third full of oil and heat to 180°C (350°F), or until a cube of bread dropped in the oil browns in 15 seconds. Deep-fry the lobster meat in two batches for 3–4 minutes, or until cooked. Remove and drain on paper towels.

To serve, put the bok choy on a plate or in a bowl, top with the lobster meat and pour the sauce over the top. Garnish with spring onions and coriander.

Stir-fried prawns with shiitake mushrooms and snow peas

10 small dried shiitake mushrooms
3 tablespoons vegetable oil
300 g (10$^1/_2$ oz) king prawns (shrimp),
peeled and deveined, tails intact
3 garlic cloves, crushed
125 g (about 20) snow peas
(mangetout), trimmed
2 tablespoons oyster sauce
3 tablespoons chicken stock*
1 tablespoon Shaoxing rice wine
$^1/_4$ teaspoon sugar

Serves 2–4

Soak the mushrooms in hot water for 30 minutes, then drain. Discard the stems. If your mushrooms are large, cut the caps in half.

Heat the oil in a hot wok. Add the prawns and stir-fry for 1 minute over high heat. Add the garlic and mushrooms and stir-fry for another 1 minute. Add the snow peas, oyster sauce, chicken stock, rice wine, sugar and a pinch of white pepper and cook for 2 minutes, or until the prawns are pink.

To serve, scoop the stir-fry into a bowl.

Stir-fried beef with eggplant and chilli

4 long green or Japanese eggplants
(aubergines)
3 tablespoons vegetable oil
4 garlic cloves, crushed
250 g (9 oz) beef fillet, finely sliced
2 long red chillies, deseeded and sliced
pinch of roasted chilli powder
2 tablespoons fish sauce
1 tablespoon sugar
2 spring onions (scallions), sliced

To serve (optional)
2 tablespoons chopped roasted peanuts*
1 handful coriander (cilantro) leaves

Serves 2–4

Cook the eggplant under a hot griller (broiler) until the skin is charred and soft. Cool the eggplant in a plastic bag, then peel off the skin and shred the flesh into strips.

Heat the oil in a hot wok. Add the garlic and stir-fry briefly (20–30 seconds) until fragrant. Add the beef and stir-fry for 1–2 minutes. Add the eggplant, chillies, chilli powder, fish sauce, sugar and a pinch of salt and cook for 1–2 minutes, or until the beef is cooked and the sauce is syrupy. Toss in the spring onions and mix well.

To serve, pile the beef mixture onto a plate, pour on the sauce and, if you want, sprinkle with peanuts and coriander.

I love this Thai method of deep-frying a whole fish and serving it with a sweet–sour sauce.

Deep-fried whole fish with three-flavoured sauce

800 g (1 lb 12 oz) whole ocean perch
or snapper
vegetable oil, for deep-frying
1 handful Thai basil leaves

Sauce
3 dried long red chillies, deseeded
3 garlic cloves, peeled
3 red Asian shallots, peeled
2 tablespoons vegetable oil
4 tablespoons shaved palm sugar
4 tablespoons tamarind water*
3 tablespoons fish sauce

Serves 2–4

Carefully make four diagonal slits across both sides of the fish, almost to the bone. Sprinkle with salt and white pepper and set aside.

To make the paste, soak the chillies in hot water for 1–2 minutes, or until softened. Remove the stems. Roughly chop. Use a mortar and pestle to pound the chillies, garlic and shallots into a paste. Alternatively, chop the ingredients into a paste using a small food processor. Heat the oil in a hot wok. Add the paste and fry until fragrant. Add the sugar, tamarind water, fish sauce, 4 tablespoons water and a pinch of salt, then reduce the heat to a simmer. Cook, stirring occasionally, for 3–4 minutes, or until the sauce becomes syrupy, then remove from the heat.

Fill a clean wok or deep-fat fryer one-half full of oil and heat to 170°C (325°F), or until a cube of bread dropped into the oil browns in 20 seconds. Carefully add the basil leaves and deep-fry until crisp—stand back when you do this as the oil will spit when the basil is added. Drain on paper towels. Reheat the oil, then carefully lower the fish into the oil. Cook the fish for 15–20 minutes, or until crisp.

To serve, put the fish on a plate. Pour the sauce over the fish and top with the fried basil.

I love lamb shanks so much that I couldn't resist using them in what is otherwise a classic Vietnamese dish.

Vietnamese braised lamb shanks

8 small (forequarter) lamb shanks, French cut
3 tablespoons vegetable oil
2 carrots, halved lengthways, then sliced into 2 cm (3/4 inch) thick slices
2 spring onions (scallions), cut into 5 cm (2 inch) lengths

Braising stock
1.25 litres (5 cups) chicken stock*
4 garlic cloves, crushed
1 onion, quartered
2 lemon grass stems, bruised
2 tablespoons sliced fresh ginger
3 star anise
4 tablespoons ground yellow bean sauce
3 tablespoons tomato paste (purée)
1 1/2 tablespoons caster (superfine) sugar

To serve
1 very small handful mint leaves
1 very small handful Vietnamese mint leaves
1 baguette

Serves 4–6

Preheat the oven to 160°C (315°F/Gas 2–3). Season the shanks with salt and white pepper. Heat the oil in a hot wok. Add the lamb shanks to the wok in two batches and fry for 2 minutes, or until browned all over. Drain on paper towels, then transfer the shanks to a deep flameproof casserole dish.

Put all the braising stock ingredients in a large saucepan and bring to the boil. Carefully pour over the shanks. Cover with a layer of baking paper, then a layer of foil. Put in the oven and braise for 3 hours, or until the shanks are tender and cooked.

Remove the shanks from the stock and keep warm. Strain the stock and discard the solids. Return the stock to the casserole dish and bring to the boil on the stovetop. Add the carrots and spring onions and simmer for 10 minutes, or until the carrots are tender. Return the shanks to the stock and cook until the shanks are piping hot.

To serve, put the lamb shanks in a serving bowl. Pour on the stock and garnish with the mint leaves. Serve with slices of baguette to dip into the sauce.

153

Stir-fried roasted duck with yellow beans, garlic and chillies

2 garlic cloves, peeled
2 long red chillies, deseeded and roughly chopped
2 tablespoons oil
1 Chinese roasted duck, boned and sliced
100 g (3¹/2 oz) water spinach, cut into 8 cm (3 inch) lengths
8 fresh baby corn, halved lengthways
3 tablespoons yellow beans, rinsed
pinch of sugar
4 tablespoons vegetable stock
1 tablespoon light soy sauce

Serves 2–4

Use a mortar and pestle to pound the garlic and chopped red chillies into a rough paste. Alternatively, chop the ingredients into a paste using a small food processor.

Heat the oil in a hot wok. Add the garlic–chilli paste and sliced duck and stir-fry for 2–3 minutes, or until fragrant. Add the water spinach, baby corn, yellow beans, sugar, stock and soy sauce and cook for about 2 minutes.

To serve, remove the duck and vegetables from the sauce and arrange on a plate. Boil the sauce until reduced by half, then pour over the duck and vegetables.

Stir-fried shredded roasted duck with chilli, bean sprouts and garlic chives

2 tablespoons vegetable oil
2 garlic cloves, crushed
¹/4 onion, sliced
1 Chinese roasted duck, boned and sliced
180 g (2 cups) bean sprouts
25 g (¹/2 bunch) garlic chives, cut into 4 cm (1¹/2 inch) lengths
2 long red chillies, deseeded and julienned
3 tablespoons chicken stock*
1 tablespoon light soy sauce
1 tablespoon Shaoxing rice wine

Serves 2–4

Heat the oil in a hot wok. Add the garlic and onion and stir-fry for 1 minute, or until fragrant. Toss in the duck and stir-fry for 1 minute. Add the bean sprouts, chives, chillies, stock, soy sauce, wine and a pinch of salt and sugar and cook for about 2 minutes. To serve, arrange on a plate and serve immediately.

This is my favourite meal. I love the earthiness of the mushrooms mixed with the sweetness of the lily buds and the crunchiness of the cloud ear fungus.

Steamed blue eye fillet with lily buds, mushrooms and noodles

20 dried lily buds
4 dried shiitake mushrooms
15 g (1/2 oz) dried cloud ear fungus
25 g (1 oz) bean thread vermicelli
2 tablespoons vegetable oil
2 garlic cloves, crushed
2 tablespoons yellow bean sauce
1 teaspoon caster (superfine) sugar
400 g (14 oz) blue eye fillet or other firm white fish fillet
1 tablespoon julienned fresh ginger

Dressing
2 tablespoons light soy sauce
1 teaspoon caster (superfine) sugar
1/4 teaspoon sesame oil
1 long red chilli, deseeded and finely sliced on the diagonal
a few coriander (cilantro) sprigs

Serves 4

In separate bowls, soak the lily buds, mushrooms and cloud ear fungus in hot water for 20–30 minutes, or until softened. Soak the bean thread vermicelli in cold water for 10 minutes. Drain them all well. Discard the stems from the mushrooms and slice the caps into strips. Roughly chop the cloud ear fungus into small pieces.

Heat the oil in a hot wok. Add the garlic and stir-fry for 10–15 seconds, or until fragrant. Remove from the heat and put into a bowl. Add the yellow bean sauce, sugar, 4 tablespoons water and a pinch of salt and pepper and mix.

Bring a wok or large saucepan of water to the boil. On a shallow plate that will fit into the steamer, combine the lily buds, bean thread vermicelli, mushrooms and fungus. Put the fish on top of the noodle mix. Pour on the yellow bean mixture, then sprinkle with the ginger. Put the plate into a steamer, then sit the steamer over the wok of boiling water, making sure the base does not touch the water. Put the lid on the steamer and cook the fish for 25–30 minutes, or until cooked through.

To make the dressing, combine the soy sauce, sugar, oil, chilli and stir until the sugar dissolves.

To serve, carefully remove the fish and noodle mixture from the steamer and drizzle the dressing over the fish. Garnish with coriander sprigs.

The French influence on Vietnamese cuisine is not to be underestimated. In Vietnam, curries such as this would be served with a baguette baked in one of the French-style bakeries that abound.

Chicken and sweet potato curry

600 g (1 lb 5 oz) chicken thigh fillet
300 g (10 1/2 oz) sweet potato, peeled and cut into 3 cm (1 1/4 inch) cubes
2 tablespoons vegetable oil
1 onion, halved and cut into thick slices
5 curry leaves
2 garlic cloves, crushed
5 cm (2 inch) knob of fresh ginger, peeled and finely grated
500 ml (2 cups) coconut milk
250 ml (1 cup) coconut cream

Marinade
8 dried long red chillies
1 tablespoon ground coriander
1/2 teaspoon ground cumin
4 white peppercorns, crushed
1 teaspoon ground turmeric

To serve
lime wedges

Serves 4

Cut the chicken into 3 cm (1 1/4 inch) pieces, then put the pieces into a non-metallic bowl.

To make the marinade, soak the chillies in hot water for 1–2 minutes, or until softened. Remove the stems and seeds. Use a mortar and pestle to pound the chillies and a pinch of salt into a fine paste. Mix in the rest of the ingredients. Alternatively, chop the ingredients into a paste using a small food processor. Scoop the marinade into the bowl with the chicken. Coat the chicken in the marinade, then leave in the refrigerator for 1 hour.

Cook the sweet potato in boiling salted water for 15–20 minutes, or until cooked, but still firm. Drain and set aside.

Heat the oil in a saucepan over low heat. Add the onion, curry leaves, garlic and ginger and fry for about 5 minutes, or until fragrant. Stir in the coconut milk and bring to the boil. Add the chicken and its marinade, then reduce the heat and simmer for 20–25 minutes, or until the chicken is nearly cooked. Add the coconut cream, sweet potato and some salt to taste, then cook for an extra 5–10 minutes, or until the chicken and sweet potato are tender.

To serve, spoon the curry into a bowl and serve with lime wedges.

Stir-fried chicken, chillies and basil

4 garlic cloves, crushed
1–3 long red chillies, roughly chopped
1–3 bird's eye chillies, roughly chopped
4 tablespoons oil
350 g (12 oz) chicken breast fillet, finely sliced
3 tablespoons chicken stock*
2 tablespoons light soy sauce
1 tablespoon dark soy sauce
2 teaspoons caster (superfine) sugar
2 handfuls Thai basil leaves

Serves 2–4

Use a mortar and pestle to pound the garlic and long and bird's eye chillies into a paste. Alternatively, chop the ingredients into a paste using a small food processor.

Heat the oil in a hot wok. Add the chilli–garlic paste and fry, stirring, for 1–2 minutes, or until fragrant. Toss in the chicken slices and stir-fry for 1–2 minutes. Add the stock, soy sauces, sugar and salt and cook for 2 minutes. Toss in the basil and cook for 30 seconds more.

To serve, pile the stir-fry into a bowl.

Chicken with cashew nuts

vegetable oil, for deep-frying
155 g (1 cup) cashew nuts
4 dried red chillies
2 garlic cloves, crushed
3 spring onions (scallions), cut into 5 cm (2 inch) lengths
400 g (14 oz) chicken breast fillet, sliced
2 tablespoons fish sauce
1 tablespoon kecap manis

To serve
2 tablespoons coriander (cilantro) leaves

Serves 2–4

Fill a wok or deep-fat fryer one-third full of oil and heat to 160°C (315°F), or until a cube of bread dropped into the oil browns in 30–35 seconds. Deep-fry the cashew nuts for 20–30 seconds. Remove and drain. Add the dried red chillies and deep-fry for 15–20 seconds. Lift out of the wok and drain. Cut the chillies in half crossways. Clean out the wok, reserving 3 tablespoons of the oil.

Heat the reserved oil in a hot wok. Add the garlic, spring onions and chicken and stir-fry for about 4 minutes, or until the chicken is nearly cooked. Add the chillies and cashew nuts, fish sauce and kecap manis and stir-fry for another 1 minute.

To serve, pile the chicken and cashew nuts onto a plate. Sprinkle with coriander leaves.

third

third

When I opened my first restaurant I wanted to offer some desserts, but found that there were very few traditional Asian desserts to choose from. This is partly because Asian sweets are more of a snack than a dessert and partly because throughout most of Asia the typical after-dinner treat is fresh fruit. I started reading cookbook after cookbook, researching desserts from around the world. The classic French and Italian desserts based on rich, creamy custards captivated my imagination. I soon started experimenting with these classic recipes by adding tropical flavours to them.

Many of the recipes in this chapter are derived from those original experiments—they use Asian flavourings, such as coconut, pandanus, banana and other tropical fruits, in a new way. I've also taken inspiration from Asian sweet snacks and made them part of a richer, more substantial dessert.

Opening a fresh coconut can be a daunting task for the inexperienced. If you do have the skill and patience to tackle a whole coconut, serve this dessert with lightly roasted fresh shards, but otherwise use roasted shredded coconut.

Coconut crème caramel

Caramel
160 g (3/4 cup) caster (superfine) sugar
125 ml (1/2 cup) water

Custard
300 ml (101/2 fl oz) single (pouring) cream
375 ml (11/2 cups) coconut milk
110 g (1/2 cup) sugar
1 teaspoon natural vanilla extract
3 egg yolks
3 eggs

To serve
4 x 12 cm (5 inch) square pieces of banana leaf
40 g (1/2 cup) roasted shredded coconut*
or roasted curls of fresh coconut

Serves 8

Preheat the oven to 150°C (300°F/Gas 2). To make the caramel, combine the sugar and water in a saucepan and stir to dissolve. Bring to the boil, then reduce the heat and cook, without stirring, for 6–12 minutes, or until the sugar starts to caramelize and turn the colour of honey. Take the pan off the heat and, working quickly, pour the caramel into eight 125 ml (1/2-cup) moulds, turning the moulds so the caramel coats the base and side.

To make the custard, combine the cream, coconut milk, sugar and vanilla extract in a saucepan over medium heat. Heat gently but don't allow to boil. In a bowl, beat the egg yolks and the eggs together. Slowly pour the cream mixture into the eggs, stirring continuously. Now pour the mixture through a fine sieve into a large bowl.

Put the caramel-lined moulds into a roasting tin. Pour enough hot water into the tin to reach halfway up the sides of the moulds. Divide the custard among each mould and bake for about 1 hour, or until just firm to the touch. Remove the moulds from the roasting tin and allow to cool. Cover and refrigerate for at least 6 hours.

To serve, run a sharp knife around the edge of the custards. Upturn each mould on a piece of banana leaf in the middle of a serving plate and top with roasted coconut.

I don't drink much, but I do love Frangelico, particularly served over ice. Here, Frangelico is transformed into a sophisticated jelly and served with fluffy peaks of coconut sauce.

Frangelico jelly with coconut sauce

750 ml (3 cups) Frangelico
4 teaspoons powdered gelatine

To serve
1 quantity coconut sauce*
mint leaves, to garnish (optional)

Serves 8

Pour the Frangelico into a large saucepan and bring slowly to the boil to burn off the alcohol. Allow to cool a little.

Put 3 tablespoons water into a small bowl and sprinkle on the gelatine evenly. Leave the gelatine to sponge and swell. Add the sponged liquid to the Frangelico and stir until completely dissolved. Pour the mixture through a fine sieve into a bowl. Cover and refrigerate until set.

To serve, break up the jelly and place in the bases of small shot glasses, then top with coconut sauce and a mint leaf. Spoon any leftover coconut sauce into a bowl and put in the middle of the table.

Colour is one of the most important elements of any food, which is why I love this dessert so much. The vibrant pink of the pomegranate, snowy white of the lychee and sunny yellow of the mango complement each other perfectly. Pomegranates only have a short season, so when they're not available experiment with raspberries or strawberries instead. To obtain the juice from a pomegranate, cut it in half across the middle, then squeeze in a juicer. For the second layer of seeds, release them into a bowl and squash them with a spoon. Strain through a sieve and add to the rest of the juice.

Trio of sorbets

Pomegranate sorbet
300 ml (10¹/₂ fl oz) water
300 g (10¹/₂ oz) caster (superfine) sugar
600 ml (21 fl oz) pomegranate juice (you'll need to squeeze 12–16 pomegranates)
3 tablespoons lemon juice

Lychee sorbet
250 ml (1 cup) water
250 g (9 oz) caster (superfine) sugar
600 ml (21 fl oz) puréed tinned lychees (you'll need 1 large and 1 small tin of lychees)
2 tablespoons lemon juice

Mango sorbet
250 ml (1 cup) water
250 g (9 oz) caster (superfine) sugar
600 ml (21 fl oz) tinned mango purée or 5–6 fresh mangoes, flesh puréed
2 tablespoons lemon juice

To serve
mint sprigs

Serves 6

Make each sorbet separately. Pour the water into a saucepan with the sugar and bring slowly to the boil, ensuring the sugar dissolves completely. Remove the pan from the heat and leave to cool. Refrigerate until completely chilled. Meanwhile, pour the fruit purée or juice through a fine sieve.

Combine the sugar syrup with the sieved purée or juice. Taste for sweetness and adjust with lemon juice, as necessary. Churn the mixture in an ice-cream machine according to the manufacturer's instructions. Transfer the sorbets to separate freezer-proof containers and freeze until ready to use.

Alternatively, if you do not have an ice-cream machine, pour each sorbet mixture into a separate shallow metal tin and freeze for 3–6 hours, or until it is just frozen around the edges. Working quickly, transfer the frozen mixture to a large bowl and beat with electric beaters until smooth. Pour the mixture back into the tray and refreeze. Repeat this step three times in total. For the final freezing, place in an airtight container and cover the surface with a piece of greaseproof paper and a lid.

Deep-fried banana fritters are a popular snack in Asia. There they would use tiny sugar bananas, which are very, very sweet. As sugar bananas are difficult to source outside Asia, this recipe uses delicate lady's finger bananas instead.

Banana fritters with honey caramel and coconut ice cream

8 small ripe lady's finger bananas, peeled
vegetable oil, for deep-frying

Ice cream
500 ml (2 cups) single (pouring) cream
500 ml (2 cups) coconut milk
4 tablespoons roasted shredded coconut*
12 egg yolks
200 g (7 oz) caster (superfine) sugar

Honey caramel
150 g (5$^{1}/_{2}$ oz) shaved palm sugar
200 ml (7 fl oz) single (pouring) cream
150 ml (5 fl oz) honey

Batter
125 g (1 cup) plain (all-purpose) flour
90 g ($^{1}/_{2}$ cup) rice flour
2 teaspoons baking powder
$^{1}/_{2}$ teaspoon salt
2 tablespoons roasted sesame seeds*

Serves 8

To make the coconut ice cream, combine the cream, coconut milk and roasted shredded coconut in a saucepan. Bring to the boil, then reduce the heat and simmer for 10 minutes. Put the egg yolks and sugar into a large heatproof bowl, then whisk using an electric whisk until pale and creamy. Strain the cream mixture into the egg mixture. Place the bowl over a saucepan of simmering water, making sure the bowl does not touch the water. Stir the mixture until it thickens and coats the back of the spoon. Lift the bowl of custard into a sink or large bowl of iced water and allow the custard to cool. Pour the custard into an ice-cream machine and churn according to the manufacturer's instructions. Transfer the ice cream to a freezer-proof container and freeze until ready to use.

Alternatively, if you do not have an ice-cream machine, pour the custard into a shallow metal tin and freeze for 3–6 hours, or until the mixture is just frozen around the edges. Working quickly, transfer the creamy mixture to a large bowl and beat with electric beaters until it is smooth. Pour the mixture back into the tray and refreeze. Repeat this step three times in total. For the final freezing, place the ice cream in an airtight container and cover the surface with a piece of greaseproof paper and a lid.

To make the honey caramel, combine the sugar, cream and honey in a saucepan. Bring to a simmer, then lower the heat and stir until the sauce becomes thick and syrupy. Remove from the heat and set aside.

To make the batter, combine all the ingredients in a large bowl, adding enough water to make a thick, smooth batter. Fill a wok one-third full of oil and heat to 180°C (350°F), or until a cube of bread dropped into the oil browns in 15 seconds. Dip each banana into the batter and deep-fry for 3 minutes, or until crisp and golden brown. Drain on crumpled paper towels.

To serve, place one banana fritter onto each plate, drizzle with honey caramel sauce and serve with coconut ice cream.

Sago is quite bland, but its starchy texture is a good base to which you can add whatever flavours you like, in this case, sweet–sour pineapple in a syrupy caramel sauce.

Taro sago pudding with pineapple in caramel sauce

300 g (10½ oz) taro, diced
150 g (5½ oz) caster (superfine) sugar
300 g (1½ cups) sago

Pineapple in caramel sauce
150 g (1 cup) coconut sugar
170 ml (⅔ cup) water
400 g (14 oz) pineapple pieces

Serves 6

Put the taro in a saucepan and just cover with water. Bring to the boil, then reduce the heat and simmer for about 7 minutes, or until the taro is tender. Remove from the heat and drain. Combine the taro and sugar and mix well. Then use a fork to mash the taro into the sugar. Set aside.

Bring the sago and 3.5 litres (14 cups) water slowly to the boil. Reduce the heat and simmer gently, stirring occasionally, for 10–15 minutes, or until it is almost clear. Remove the pan from the heat and sit for 10 minutes, or until it is completely clear. Drain through a fine sieve and rinse under water for about 15 seconds to remove a little of the starch (don't rinse out all the starch as some is needed to hold the pudding together). Drain well. Stir the sago into the taro mixture, then ladle into six 125 ml (½-cup) ramekins or one large 750 ml (3-cup) mould. Cover and refrigerate overnight.

To make the caramel sauce, put the coconut sugar and water in a saucepan and stir over medium heat until the sugar dissolves. Increase the heat and bring to the boil, then cook, without stirring, for 5–6 minutes, or until a rich caramel colour develops. Remove from the heat, then stir in the pineapple. Set aside.

To serve, scoop some of the pineapple onto the pudding and drizzle with the caramel sauce.

In China, mung bean dumplings are a celebration food, served at weddings, birthdays and New Year. More commonly made into a savoury dish, they are versatile enough to be served as a sweet.

Mung bean dumplings with ginger and cinnamon broth

60 g (1/4 cup) mung beans
1 tablespoon sugar
100 g (3/4 cup) glutinous rice flour
4 tablespoons warm water

Broth
540 g (3 cups) chopped palm sugar
6 cinnamon sticks
16 slices fresh ginger

To serve
2 teaspoons roasted white sesame seeds*

Serves 4–6

Soak the mung beans in cold water for 1 hour, then drain. Put the mung beans in a saucepan with 750 ml (3 cups) water. Bring to the boil. Reduce the heat and simmer for 20–25 minutes, or until the beans are tender. Drain well. Put in a bowl with the sugar and a pinch of salt and mash. Leave to cool, then shape into balls—you should get around twelve.

Combine the flour and most of the warm water and mix to a soft but firm dough, adding the remaining water if necessary. Knead well on a floured surface, then shape into as many balls as you have mung bean balls. Flatten each ball into a 6 cm (2 1/2 inch) disc with floured fingers, then wrap around the mung bean mixture and seal. Shake off any excess flour. Bring 3 litres (12 cups) water to the boil. Carefully drop a few dumplings at time into the water and cook for 2–3 minutes, or until the dumplings float to the surface. Remove using a slotted spoon and refresh under cold water. Drain well and set aside.

To make the broth, put all the ingredients and 1.25 litres (5 cups) water in a saucepan and bring to the boil, stirring to dissolve the sugar. Reduce the heat to low and simmer for 20 minutes to infuse all the flavours and until the broth becomes syrupy. Add the dumplings and cook for 10 minutes.

To serve, divide the dumplings among serving bowls, ladle on some broth and garnish with a cinnamon stick and some sesame seeds.

177

Here I've taken a well-known Italian dessert and added an exotic twist by infusing the custard with the delicate floral fragrance of the pandanus leaf.

Pandanus panna cotta with mango and passionfruit

4 teaspoons gelatine powder
250 ml (1 cup) milk
70 g (2¹/2 oz) caster (superfine) sugar
1 pandanus leaf, tied in a knot
¹/2 vanilla bean, split lengthways
400 ml (14 fl oz) single (pouring) cream

Mango and passionfruit
2 small or 1 large mango, diced
250 g (1 cup) passionfruit pulp
(about 8 passionfruit)

To serve
mint leaves

Serves 6

Put 3 tablespoons of water into a small bowl and sprinkle on the gelatine evenly. Leave the gelatine to sponge and swell.

Put the milk, sugar, pandanus leaf and vanilla bean in a small saucepan. Bring to a very gentle simmer, then simmer for 10 minutes to infuse the flavours, but be careful not to boil the milk. Remove from the heat and leave to infuse for another 10 minutes. Discard the pandanus leaf.

Add the sponged liquid to the milk and stir until completely dissolved. Strain the warm milk into a bowl through a fine sieve and refrigerate until half set. Whip the cream until soft peaks form. Gently fold the whipped cream into the milk mixture and pour into six 125 ml (¹/2-cup) dariole moulds. Refrigerate until set.

Combine the mangoes and passionfruit and mix well.

To serve, briefly dip the base of the dariole moulds into warm water, then turn the panna cotta out onto individual serving plates. Drizzle with the mango and passionfruit and garnish with a mint leaf.

In Vietnam this pudding is normally steamed, whereas in Thailand it is usually grilled.

Banana sticky rice pudding with coconut sauce

400 g (2 cups) glutinous rice
500 ml (2 cups) coconut cream
5 tablespoons sugar
40 g (1/2 cup) roasted shredded coconut*
8 rectangular pieces of banana leaf, each 15 x 25 cm (6 x 10 inches)
8 small ripe lady's finger bananas, peeled

To serve
1 quantity coconut sauce*
3 tablespoons ground roasted peanuts*
2 tablespoons roasted sesame seeds*

Serves 8

Put the rice, coconut cream, sugar, coconut, a pinch of salt and 125 ml (1/2 cup) water in a saucepan. Bring to the boil, then reduce the heat and simmer, stirring frequently, for 10 minutes, or until all the liquid has been absorbed. It is important to stir the mixture as it is very thick and may burn very quickly. Set aside and allow to cool.

Blanch the banana leaves in boiling water until bright green and pliant. Take each leaf and place about 2 tablespoons of the rice mixture along one edge. You may find it easier if you wet your hand. Top the rice with a banana, then cover the banana with another 2 tablespoons of rice. Fold both sides of the leaf over the rice, then roll the whole thing over to form a package. Secure the packages with string.

Bring a wok or large saucepan of water to the boil. Put the banana leaf packages into a large steamer—you may need to do this in batches. Sit the steamer over the wok of boiling water, making sure the base of the steamer does not touch the water. Put the lid on the steamer and steam the packages for 15 minutes, or until cooked through.

To serve, place the unwrapped banana pudding onto serving plates. Pour some coconut sauce over the top and sprinkle with ground roasted peanuts and roasted sesame seeds.

In most Asian countries cassava is the cheapest staple food, so it is not held in high regard. I like it because it's a great sponge for other flavours. Outside Asia it can be difficult to find fresh, so if you have trouble, buy frozen and thaw it before using.

Baked cassava cake with coconut sauce

100 g (3^1/$_2$ oz) butter, melted
600 g (1 lb 5 oz) cassava, finely grated and excess water squeezed out
250 ml (1 cup) coconut cream
230 g (1 cup) caster (superfine) sugar
2 eggs, lightly beaten

To serve
1 quantity coconut sauce*
2 tablespoons ground roasted peanuts*
2 tablespoons roasted sesame seeds*

Serves 8–10

Preheat the oven to 180°C (350°F/Gas 4). Combine all the ingredients in a bowl and mix well. Leave to settle for 10–15 minutes. Pour the mixture into a 20 cm (8 inch) non-stick springform cake tin and smooth the surface. Bake for 45–50 minutes, or until cooked.

Warm the coconut sauce in a saucepan over low heat.

To serve, place a wedge of cake onto a pool of warm coconut sauce and sprinkle with peanuts and sesame seeds.

basics+glossary

basics

★ The following basic recipes are marked with a star* when they are referred to in the book.

Black vinegar dressing

3 tablespoons grapeseed oil
3 tablespoons black vinegar
1 tablespoon light soy sauce
pinch of sugar

Makes 125 ml (1/2 cup)

Combine all the ingredients in a bowl and mix well.

Caramel syrup

300 g (10 1/2 oz) chopped dark
    palm sugar

Makes 250 ml (1 cup)

Put the sugar and 150 ml (5 fl oz) water in a saucepan and bring to the boil. Reduce the heat and simmer for 4 minutes, or until it reaches the consistency of syrup.

Chicken stock

2 kg (4 lb 8 oz) chicken carcasses
2 slices of fresh ginger
2 spring onions (scallions), roughly
    chopped

Remove any fat from the chicken carcasses and clean under cold

water. Put all the ingredients into a stockpot or large saucepan with 3 litres (12 cups) water. Bring to the boil, then reduce the heat and simmer gently. Skim off any scum and fat that rises to the surface during cooking.

Cook the stock for 2–2 1/2 hours. Cool for about 10 minutes, then strain the stock through a fine sieve and discard any solids. Store the stock in the refrigerator for up to 3 days or freeze for up to 6 months.

Chilli jam

60 g (1/2 cup) dried shrimp
40 dried long red chillies
vegetable oil, for deep-frying
12 red Asian shallots, sliced
    lengthways
20 garlic cloves, sliced lengthways
4 tablespoons fish sauce
85 g (3 oz) shaved palm sugar
2 tablespoons tamarind paste

Makes about 250 ml (1 cup)

Soak the dried shrimp in hot water for 10–15 minutes, or until softened. Drain, then dry thoroughly. Soak the chillies in hot water for 1–2 minutes, then drain. Pat dry. Remove the stems and seeds, then chop.

Fill a wok or deep-fat fryer one-third full of oil and heat to 180°C (350°F), or until a cube of bread dropped into the oil browns in 15 seconds. Cooking each ingredient separately, deep-fry the shallots, garlic, dried

chillies and dried shrimp until golden. Drain on paper towels. Allow the oil to cool a little. Use a mortar and pestle to pound the deep-fried shallots, garlic, chillies and shrimp into a paste with 4–5 tablespoons of the oil from the wok. Alternatively, chop the ingredients into a paste using a small food processor. In a hot wok, bring the mixture to the boil and season with the fish sauce, palm sugar and tamarind paste. Reduce the heat and simmer, stirring regularly, until quite thick. Remove and allow to cool. Store in an airtight jar for up to 3 weeks in the fridge.

Coconut sauce

1 tablespoon cornflour (cornstarch)
500 ml (2 cups) coconut cream
1 pandanus leaf, trimmed, then tied
    into a knot and bruised
4 tablespoons caster (superfine)
    sugar

Makes 500 ml (2 cups)

Mix the cornflour into 3 tablespoons water and set aside.

Put the coconut cream, pandanus leaf, sugar and a pinch of salt in a saucepan and bring to the boil. Reduce the heat and simmer gently for 3 minutes to allow the pandanus leaf to flavour the coconut cream. Remove the pandanus leaf, then slowly stir the cornflour mixture into the coconut mixture, stirring constantly until the sauce starts to thicken. Remove from the heat.

Fried shallots

16–20 red Asian shallots, finely
  sliced
vegetable oil, for deep-frying

Makes 100 g (1 cup)

Fill a wok or deep-fat fryer one-third
full of oil and heat to 160°C (315°F),
or until a cube of bread dropped
into the oil browns in 30–35 seconds.
Carefully add all the shallots,
standing back as the oil may splash
and bubble up. Deep-fry, stirring
occasionally, for 1 minute, or until
crisp, then drain on crumpled paper
towels. Keeps for 2 days in an
airtight container.

Ground roasted rice

4 tablespoons glutinous (sticky) rice

Makes 50 g (1/4 cup)

Dry-fry the rice in a frying pan over
low heat, stirring regularly until
golden brown and fragrant. The rice
must smell nutty and roasted.
Leave to cool, then use a mortar
and pestle or spice grinder to grind
to a fine powder.

Herb salt

2 tablespoons coriander seeds
2 tablespoons salt

Makes 80 g (1/3 cup)

Use a mortar and pestle or spice
grinder to grind the coriander into a
fine powder. Mix it with the salt until
well blended.

Hoisin dressing

3 tablespoons hoisin sauce
2 tablespoons light soy sauce
1 tablespoon rice vinegar
1 1/2 tablespoons honey
1/4 teaspoon sesame oil

Makes 125 ml (1/2 cup)

Combine all ingredients in a bowl.
Stir until all the ingredients are
well mixed.

Master stock

8 cm (3 inch) knob of fresh ginger,
  sliced
250 ml (1 cup) light soy sauce
250 ml (1 cup) Shaoxing rice wine
200 g (7 oz) rock sugar
5 garlic cloves, crushed
5 star anise
3 cinnamon sticks
2 pieces dried orange peel

Makes 4 litres (16 cups)

Put all the ingredients with 3 litres
(12 cups) water in a stockpot or
large saucepan and bring to the
boil. Reduce the heat to a gentle
simmer for 15 minutes to allow the
spices to infuse. Strain.

Nuoc cham

2 long red chillies, deseeded
  and roughly chopped
1 garlic clove, peeled
1 tablespoon shaved palm sugar
2 tablespoons lime juice
3 tablespoons fish sauce
1 tablespoon rice vinegar

Makes 200 ml (7 fl oz)

Use a mortar and pestle to pound
the chillies and garlic into a paste.
Alternatively, chop the ingredients
into a paste using a small food
processor. Add the palm sugar,
lime juice, fish sauce, vinegar and
3 tablespoons water. Stir until the
sugar dissolves.

Pepper and salt mix

3 tablespoons salt
1 tablespoon white pepper

Makes 80 g (1/3 cup)

Combine the salt and pepper and
stir until well blended. Store in an
airtight container.

Roasted peanuts/ cashew nuts

160 g (1 cup) unsalted peanuts
or cashew nuts

Makes 160 g (1 cup)

Dry-fry the nuts in a frying pan over low heat, stirring regularly until the peanuts are lightly roasted on the outside and cooked through. Store in an airtight container in the refrigerator for up to 3 months. Grind or chop as needed.

Sweet chilli sauce

3 garlic cloves, peeled
3 long red chillies, roughly chopped
500 ml (2 cups) rice vinegar
330 g (1$1/2$ cups) sugar

Makes 750 ml (3 cups)

Use a mortar and pestle to pound the garlic and chillies into a paste. Alternatively, chop the ingredients into a paste using a small food processor. Combine all the ingredients and 500 ml (2 cups) water and 1 teaspoon salt in a saucepan and bring to boil. Reduce the heat, then simmer until reduced by half, or until the mixture thickens to a slightly syrupy consistency. Remove and allow to cool.

Roasted sesame seeds

2 tablespoons sesame seeds

Makes 2 tablespoons

Dry-fry the sesame seeds in a frying pan over low heat, stirring regularly until the seeds swell and are lightly roasted but not burnt.

Roasted shredded coconut

40 g ($1/2$ cup) dry shredded coconut

Makes 40 g ($1/2$ cup)

Dry-fry the coconut in a frying pan over medium–low heat, stirring regularly until the coconut swells and is lightly roasted.

Tamarind paste

100 g (3$1/2$ oz) seedless
tamarind pulp
100 ml (3$1/2$ fl oz) hot water

Makes 150 g ($1/2$ cup)

Cover the tamarind with hot water for 15–20 minutes. Squeeze and work to dissolve it. Strain the liquid through a sieve and discard the fibre. Store in an airtight container in the refrigerator for up to 5 days.

Tamarind water

100 g (3$1/2$ oz) seedless
tamarind pulp
300 ml (10$1/2$ fl oz) hot water

Makes 300 ml (10$1/2$ fl oz)

Cover the tamarind with hot water for 15–20 minutes. Squeeze and work to dissolve it. Strain the liquid through a sieve and discard the fibre. Store in an airtight container in the refrigerator for up to 5 days.

glossary

bamboo shoots The edible shoots of bamboo. Available fresh when in season, otherwise preserved in jars or tinned. Fresh shoots should be blanched if they are bitter.

banana blossom The purple, teardrop-shaped flower of the banana plant. Only the inner pale core is eaten and this needs to be soaked before use. Wear rubber gloves to prepare the blossom as it has a gummy substance that can stain.

banana leaf Large green leaves, which can be used as a wrapping for foods, or to line plates. Available from Asian shops.

bean curd *see* tofu.

bean thread vermicelli These are very thin white translucent noodles that turn clear when soaked. They are much tougher than rice noodles.

black/yellow beans Fermented and salted soya beans, usually available tinned. Rinse them before use.

black vinegar A richly flavoured vinegar made from glutinous (sticky) rice.

char siu (Chinese barbecued pork) A pork fillet that has been marinated, then barbecued over charcoal. Available from Chinese barbecue shops.

chilli Generally, the smaller the Asian chilli the hotter it is. Bird's eye chillies are the smallest and hottest. Dried red chillies are often soaked in hot water to soften them. Remove the seeds if you prefer less heat.

chilli bean sauce Made from soya beans fermented with chillies, salt and sometimes garlic. There are many varieties available, all slightly different.

chilli jam A thick, chilli relish that can also be used as a sauce. Make it yourself (see page 185) or buy it ready-made.

Chinese broccoli This plant has green leaves and small white flowers. Young stalks are crisp and mild; thicker stalks need to be halved. Also known as gai lan.

Chinese cabbage Shaped like a cos lettuce, this pale cabbage has tightly packed leaves and a delicate flavour. Also known as wom bok.

choy sum The smooth green leaves and pale stems have a light, sweet mustardy flavour.

cloud ear fungus A funghi that is available fresh and dried, this has a cartilaginous texture and very little flavour. Dried fungus is soaked before use. Also called black fungus and wood ear.

coconut cream This is made by soaking freshly grated coconut in boiling water, then squeezing out a thick, sweet coconut-flavoured liquid. It is available tinned.

coconut milk A thinner version of coconut cream, made as above but with more water or from a second pressing. Available tinned.

coconut sugar The sugar is made from the sap from coconut trees. Palm sugar or unrefined soft brown sugar can be used instead.

coriander or cilantro Fresh coriander leaves are used both as an ingredient and as a garnish. The roots are chopped or ground and used in curry pastes and sauces. The round seeds have a spicy aroma and are used in curry pastes. They are available whole or ground.

cumin seeds The elongated ridged seeds of a plant of the parsley family, these have a peppery, slightly bitter flavour. Available whole or ground.

curry leaves Small, pointed leaves with a spicy, toasty curry flavour. Widely used in Malay cooking.

daikon A large white radish with firm, crisp flesh and a mild flavour.

dried shrimp These are either ground until they form a fine fluff or rehydrated and used whole. Look for dark pink ones.

fish sauce Made from salted anchovy-like fish that are left to break down naturally in the heat, fish sauce is literally the liquid that is drained off.

galangal A rhizome, similar to ginger.

garlic chives These have a long, flat leaf and a garlicky taste. Used as a vegetable.

ginger The rhizome of a tropical plant which is sold in knobs. Fresh young ginger should have a smooth, pinkish beige skin and be firm and juicy. As it ages, the skin toughens and the flesh becomes more fibrous. Avoid old, wrinkled ginger as it will be tough. Ginger is often measured in centimetre (inch) pieces and this means pieces with an average-sized width.

glutinous (sticky) rice A short-grain rice that cooks to a sticky mass. Glutinous rice is labelled as such and has plump, highly polished and shiny grains.

hoisin sauce A sweet-spicy Chinese sauce made from soya beans, garlic, sugar and spices.

lap cheong (Chinese sausage) An air-dried spicy pork sausage.

lemon grass The fibrous stem of a citrus-perfumed grass, it is finely chopped or sliced or cut into chunks. Discard the outer layers until you reach the softer, white part.

lily buds The unopened buds of a type of lily. Also called golden needles.

lotus stem These are the crunchy stems of an aquatic member of the water lily family. Outside Asia they are more commonly available in jars. If fresh, peel the stems before use.

lychees Small round fruit with a red leathery skin and translucent white flesh surrounding a brown stone. Very perfumed and often available peeled and seeded in a syrup as a dessert.

makrut (kaffir) limes These knobbly skinned fruit are used for their zest. The leaves are double leaves with a fragrant citrus oil. They are used very finely shredded or torn into large pieces. Frozen leaves are available but are less fragrant than fresh ones.

mirin A sweet spirit-based rice liquid.

mung beans Whole beans are puréed or ground and used in desserts. Also used to make bean thread vermicelli.

mustard greens A strong bitter cabbage that is generally pickled. Also called gai choy.

noodles Rice noodles are made of rice flour and water and steamed in sheets before being cut into widths. They are sold fresh and dried. The widths can be used interchangeably. Wheat noodles are usually made with egg.

palm sugar Palm sugar is made by boiling sugar palm sap until it turns into a granular paste. Sold in hard cakes of varying sizes or as a slightly softer version in tubs. Unrefined, soft light brown sugar can be used instead.

pandanus leaves These long green leaves are shaped like blades and are used as a flavouring in desserts and sweets. The leaves are often sold frozen. Pandanus are also called screwpine.

red Asian shallots Small reddish-purple shallots used in South-East Asia. French shallots can be used instead.

rice flour Made from white and black rice, this is also known as ground rice and is used in desserts.

rice vinegar Made from vinegar and a natural rice extract.

roasted chilli powder Both bird's eye and sky-pointing chillies are used to make chilli powder. Buy from Asian food

shops or make your own by roasting and grinding whole chillies.

sago Small dried balls of sago palm sap, which are used for milky desserts and savoury dishes. Cooked sago is transparent and soft with a silky texture.

rock sugar Uneven lumps of sugar, which may need to be further crushed before use. It is a pure sugar that makes sauces shiny and clear. You can use sugar lumps instead.

sesame oil An aromatic oil made from roasted sesame seeds. Use sparingly as it has a very strong, rich flavour.

Shaoxing rice wine Chinese rice wine made from glutinous (sticky) rice.

shiitake mushrooms Used both fresh and dried. Dried ones need to be soaked in hot water before use.

shredded coconut Flakes of sweet, moist coconut.

shrimp paste A strong smelling dark brownish-pink paste made from salted, fermented and dried shrimp. Used as it is or roasted first and refrigerated. Available in blocks or jars.

snake bean A long, green, stringless bean. Also called longbean.

soy sauce Dark soy sauce is sweeter than Chinese-style soy sauce.

spring roll wrappers Wheat and egg dough wrappers that can be bought from Asian food shops and some good supermarkets. Look in the refrigerator or freezer sections. Squares of filo can also be used.

star anise A star shaped Chinese fruit made up of eight segments. They are sun-dried until hard and brown, and have an aniseed flavour.

sugar cane These thick canes look similar to bamboo shoots. They are usually found tinned.

tamarind A fruit whose flesh is used as a souring agent. Usually bought as a dried cake or prepared as a purée, tamarind is actually a pod filled with seeds and a fibrous flesh. If you buy tamarind cake, then it must be soaked in hot water and then rubbed and squeezed to dissolve the pulp around the fibres. The fibres are then sieved out. Pulp is sold as purée or concentrate.

taro The name for a family of tropical tubers, and a staple in Asia. The skin is brown and the flesh ranges from white and pink to purple. Raw taro is indigestible; cook it before eating.

Thai apple eggplant (aubergine) Small, light green eggplants with a firm flesh.

Thai basil A herb with purplish stems, green leaves and an aniseed aroma and flavour.

tofu Also called bean curd, this can be firm or silken (soft).

turmeric A rhizome like ginger and galangal. Often used as a powder.

water chestnuts These are small, rounded, crisp vegetables, usually sold tinned, but sometimes available fresh. Fresh water chestnuts must be peeled.

watercress An aquatic plant, a type of cress, that is both cultivated and found growing in the wild. Its dark-green leaves have a peppery, slightly mustardy flavour.

water spinach Also called kang kong, morning glory, ong choy and water convolvulus, this is a leafy green vegetable that has hollow stems.

won ton skins These skins or wrappers are available from the refrigerator or freezer cabinets of Asian food shops. Some are yellow and include egg in the pastry and others are white.

yellow bean sauce This salty paste is made of yellow soya beans.

yellow beans see black beans

index